PRETTY LITTLE THINGS

collage jewelry   trinkets   keepsakes

N

NORTH LIGHT BOOKS
CINCINNATI, OHIO
www.artistsnetwork.com

Sally Jean
Alexander

10 09 08 07 06   5 4 3 2 1

Distributed in Canada by Fraser Direct
100 Armstrong Avenue
Georgetown, ON, Canada L7G 5S4
Tel: (905) 877-4411

Distributed in the U.K. and Europe
by David & Charles
Brunel House, Forde Close, Newton Abbot,
Devon, TQ12 4PU, England
Tel: (+44) 1626 323200, Fax: (+44) 1626 323319
Email: postmaster@davidandcharles.co.uk

Distributed in Australia by Capricorn Link Pty.
P.O. Box 704, S. Windsor NSW 2756 Australia
Tel: (+61) 02 4577-3555

Library of Congress Cataloging-in-Publication Data
Alexander, Sally Jean.
  Pretty little things : collage jewelry, keepsakes,
  and trinkets /
  Sally Jean Alexander.-- 1st ed.
    p. cm.
  Includes bibliographical references and index.
  ISBN-13: 978-1-58180-842-1 (pbk. : alk. paper)
  ISBN-10: 1-58180-842-9 (pbk. : alk. paper)
  1. Collage. I. Title.
  TT910.A54 2006
  702.81'2--dc22
                    2006005807

Editor: Tonia Davenport
Designer: Marissa Bowers
Photo Stylist: Jan Nickum
Photographers: Christine Polomsky and Al Parrish
Production Coordinator: Greg Nock

METRIC CONVERSION CHART

TO CONVERT	TO	MULTIPLY BY
Inches	Centimeters	2.54
Centimeters	Inches	0.4
Feet	Centimeters	30.5
Centimeters	Feet	0.03
Yards	Meters	0.9
Meters	Yards	1.1
Sq. Inches	Sq. Centimeters	6.45
Sq. Centimeters	Sq. Inches	0.16
Sq. Feet	Sq. Meters	0.09
Sq. Meters	Sq. Feet	10.8
Sq. Yards	Sq. Meters	0.8
Sq. Meters	Sq. Yards	1.2
Pounds	Kilograms	0.45
Kilograms	Pounds	2.2
Ounces	Grams	28.3
Grams	Ounces	0.035

to Mom and Dad who never stopped Believing in me. not For one moment. ever.

to nANNy. Who under stood me And loved me any way. I Miss you every day.

to Brad my husband Who tolerates my mooD Swings, OBsession with keeping Stuff for ever and lemon drop fetish. "Yes," you are my SouL mate

And most especially to My 3 children

elliOT I love You for speaKing French on DeMand, not laughing At me when I cry DUring every movie, and maKing me proud every day. and I am.

to erIKa you Are mY fa-vor-ite DAUGHTER. i love you more THAN you'll Ever know. never ForGet that

To ENzo I love you, my surprise baby, for Letting me draw "Love S" On the back of your hand, your gen-tle kissEs and ENzO ART

To my bestest friends who understand my hibernation six months out of the year and love me anyway. Thank you for encouraging the artist (not manufacturer) within me.
You always have my back and I love you for it.

To my editor Tonia, whose patience is beyond comprehension. Thank you for putting up with my ". . .", fragmented sentences, and lack of ability to meet a deadline. Your support never wavered and I am grateful. Long live the fir.

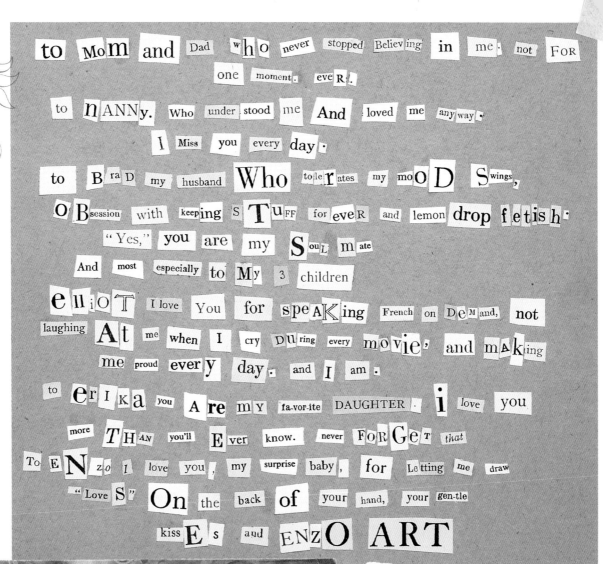

TO U2...FOR WHEN I PUT ON MY HEADpHONES YOU TAKE ME PLACES I HAVE NEVER BEEN AND tHE ART JUSt SPiLLS OUt.

Thank you from the bottom of my heart.

THE END

TABLE OF CONTENTS

SPARKLE, SMUDGE AND SHINE

Slide into your bunny slippers. Turn on the fairy lights. Curl up in a tattered, cushy chair. Covet something old. Learn something new. Welcome to my world.

There's a playground inside each of us. A silly, self-indulgent soul that hides amongst our day-to-day "trivolities" we must perform. We know it's there. We see it when our eyes catch a glimpse of a ruffled-sparkling something. We can taste it when we lick an ice cream cone covered in chocolate sprinkles. We can feel it when we close our eyes and dream. Imagine a world covered in chocolate sprinkles. Imagine being in a world surrounded by pretty little things.

Within these pages you will escape to that inner playground—a silly, sentimental journey sprinkled with a playful air and a sense of magic. Is your dream to become Queen For a Day (with a pink tiara)? Do you desire a secret way to make wishes come true (with a glittering magic wand)? Would you like to honor the generations of women before you (with a wine-glass doll)?

In our playground we will marry vintage ephemera, antique photos, found objects, scavenged text and other charming elements, in a playful, yet nostalgic way and elegantly turn existing objects into goodies you will cherish forever. In doing so, your heart will fill with joy, your home will fill with laughter, and you will rediscover that yesterday's playground can still be ever so enchanting today.

Welcome to my world of *Pretty Little Things* . . .

i am so lucky. i love my studio. love. love. love.

VISIT SALLY'S STUDIO

It all began in my kitchen, where on the tiny island I would make my hand-pressed, clay tiles. Although this space was conveniently close to Diet Coke and chocolate, I needed more space. I spilled into the breakfast area, and then transformed my formal living room into my studio. Of course, it needed to be "presentable," since it was the first room seen when entering the front door. Ugh! I can hardly keep up with my laundry let alone pick up my paints and cuttings every night.

Each home I've lived in since then has offered more and more inspirational studio space. Should my studio even be in my home? I've often debated that. But the beauty in having the place you spend so much time in be in your home is that you can run to it at a moment's notice and stay as long as you like. Creative spurts come and go. Being so close allows me to create when I feel the passion and take a break when and however often I need one.

Now my studio is just what I always dreamed it would be . . . crystal chandeliers and little fairy lights . . . white slipcovers and old chests . . . fragile things that can be broken without a second thought . . . Enzo art. I watch the sunrise outside my windows as I start my day. I peer out at my beautiful view of the city, with the trees blowing in the breeze and the rain pounding on the patio (as is often the case here in Oregon). There's a tattered, stuffed chair that is home to me when it isn't home to the studio cat(s) and Lucy, who lights my way when I get lost. It is just the place I need to whisk me away to someplace . . . well . . . artful.

But, no matter if your studio is your dining room table when the kids are at school, or an old warehouse with walls of windows and a fireplace to keep it warm, let your studio be your haven. Always have at least one very special thing there to make it yours. Perhaps it is something as small as a scented candle flickering while you create. Maybe a wall covered with pages from magazines that you gravitate to. Or a chair of your very own—one you can curl up in and sketch your ideas in your "book-book"—the one you carry with you always—just in case a creative notion pops up. Don't bring household or work issues into this place. It is your creative space—revel in it.

I surround myself with things that I love. Things that move me—really move me. I look up and see a wall covered in favorite photographs, old labels, magazine articles and jewelry. Everything that makes me smile or makes me cry. This is where I want to be surrounded by that which triggers my senses. It is here that I create. I can't help it. I put my headphones on and turn the volume up high—really high. I dance while I create. I also sing (or try to). Even my daughter and her friends have come to accept the off-key shouting from the studio (sometimes they can even make out the words) but they always giggle. After all, how talented must one be to carry a tune this poorly?

WHAT SHOULD YOU KNOW ABOUT MY STUDIO?

There's always a mess here. And there should be—it's a studio—a place to create! Even the scraps of paper that fall to the floor create a collage that inspires me.

WHAT IS MY FAVORITE COLOR?

Oh, you know that light blue with a hint of pale green, faded, aged, time-worn, sometimes chippy . . .

HOW DO I COME UP WITH MY IDEAS?

I carry a book with me everywhere—referred to as the book-book. I make them myself by vertically cutting reams of cardstock in half and binding it in 1-inch (3cm) groups. I take them with me everywhere. I might be driving down the street and see something—maybe an old parked car—and it triggers something that is completely the opposite. I'm not sure how it happens, but I write it down (or draw it). Maybe it is an item I need to source. Maybe it is a style of pendant or, maybe it's just a reminder to myself to do the laundry.

WHAT ARE THE TWO THINGS I LOVE TO CREATE WITH?

Elmer's white glue and a charcoal pencil. I've found that glue helps my antique papers stick better than gel medium. (Impatient me—I want it to stick fast.) Charcoal pencil shadows, ages and finishes off my art. It doesn't taste so good—but it looks great!

WHAT IS MY BIGGEST SECRET SOURCE?
Well, Anthropologie is a wonderful store—the clothes, the home décor, the window displays! Besides shopping there, their catalog is perfect for collage. The patterns and prints in their curtains and couches, not to mention the photo backgrounds are ideal, and the paper is just the right texture. Their offerings are so wonderful.

WHAT IS MY BIGGEST MISTAKE?
Taking my book-book to bed with me. Since ideas can pop up at any moment, it is good to have it handy. (You never know what you will dream up.) But, I always use a fine-point marker and I always fall asleep. Now my linens have black marks—which have been known to inspire me, on occasion.

Sally's Day

I wake up in the morning and the first thing I do is don my bunny slippers. But, on this particular day, Stinky is wearing them! The rat! (Actually, the cat!)

If I'm not wearing my headphones and listening to music at the highest setting, I have the TV tuned to Court TV, Fox News or MSNBC. And always, always "Abrams Report" on at 1 or 3—Pacific Time.

Lucy lights my way! She is Queen of the Candy Necklaces and makes sure every package gets one . . . it is the ultimate bling.

Pretty Anthropologie shower curtains (could they possibly be?) hide industrial shelving that holds dozens of clear plastic shoe boxes filled with assortments of flowers, paint, metal, stamps, beads, tools, glass, ribbon, etc. Each is labeled and it is a struggle (a huge one) to keep it all organized.

Where do crystal chandeliers belong? They belong in my studio! This one was a Christmas gift from my children, acquired at one of my favorite shops, Urbino. Nearby is a wind chime made by my friend Ludmil from silverware, crystals and old lamp parts. Then there's the mattress-spring candleholder . . . which just goes to show you that anything is great when hanging.

Small cubbyholes hold some of my favorite things: circa 1800s letters from France and Italy, miniature albums of tintype photos, jars of antique marbles, cabinet cards, boxes of tiny flash cards, unfinished workshop projects, and other unusual treasures. Nearby, clear organizers hold charms galore . . .each with a different collection and each compartment with a different charm. Yes, someone had a good time at Storables.

A prize find, this cabinet has sixty-eight drawers (give or take) and holds…more charms! I didn't label the drawers at first, but then (after pulling open a bunch of drawers only to find what I was looking for in the last one) I labeled each one using vintage letter stamps. The cabinet is topped by a vintage mannequin (of course she is naked, except for her tiara!) and a stack of faded berry baskets I use to sort retail orders. The color was just right! Imagine that!

Bowls of goodies abound. Here, old baby shoes, silver stars, and vintage stencils gather. They were last year's Christmas tree ornaments and looked so yummy in the bowl after I took them down that they needed to stay there.

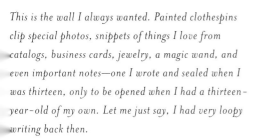

Nestled between old glass battery jars filled with ephemera is a vintage, revolving display that holds an assortment of charms. I love the way the charms shimmer when I spin it!

This is the wall I always wanted. Painted clothespins clip special photos, snippets of things I love from catalogs, business cards, jewelry, a magic wand, and even important notes—one I wrote and sealed when I was thirteen, only to be opened when I had a thirteen-year-old of my own. Let me just say, I had very loopy writing back then.

How could I be without my man statue—isn't he hot? Dan, the keeper of the brushes. He guards my dish of pale blue M&M's there when I need a sugar boost.

Isn't it funny how we usually have so many brushes . . . but use only 2 or 3 of them? That is, until we forget to rinse them out!

The true mystery of the world is the visible, not the invisible.

Oscar Wilde

Abracadabra Collage Technique

So you're stumped. Facing a blank canvas with a pile of collage supplies at the ready. What to do, what to do? Never fear—Abracadabra Collage is here! Deciding what to do is as easy as pulling a rabbit out of a hat! No, really! Just write each of the tasks on itsy-bitsy slips of paper and your answer will magically be revealed. Preset your limit (do the first ten tasks that you draw from the hat), or continue performing the tasks until you run out of slips of paper. Challenge yourself: Can you collage while blindfolded? While playing Texas Hold 'em? While drinking Strawberry Drops? Oh yes. I say you can!

special ingredients

scrap paper

pen

silver trophy cup, crystal bowl, top hat or other inspiring vessel

cardstock, watercolor paper or canvas

collage supplies (these are suggestions—use whatever inspires you)

acrylic paints and brushes

gel medium or white glue

pretty papers that you love

old books (for text)

magazines (for text or images)

photographs (vintage or current)

ink (black or colored)

chalk, oil pastels and charcoal

baby wipes

pencil

rubber stamps and inkpads

sandpaper

craft knife, scissors and awl (to both scratch and cut with)

three-dimensional objects (game pieces, beads . . .)

heat gun (for the impatient)

fingers willing to get messy . . .they will!

Want more?

Try blindfolding yourself to do the tasks you draw from the bowl. This can be quite challenging (and messy) but really, very fun. For extra credit, blindfold yourself AND collage behind your back!

1 *List.*

Write the following list of tasks three times on paper and tear the paper into separate pieces: PAINT, MAGAZINE, TEXT, PAPER, CHALK, PASTELS, CHARCOAL, PENCIL, STAMP, SCRATCH, WIPE, INK, PATTERN, 3-D, WRITE, PHOTOGRAPH, SMUDGE, DRAW, SAND, SURPRISE, and anything else you can think of! Place the torn papers into your chosen vessel and mix them up.

2 *Paint.*

Lay out a piece of cardstock, watercolor paper, or canvas that is the size of collage you wish to create. Draw a slip of paper out of the bowl (no peeking!) and do what it says: PAINT. Apply acrylic paints haphazardly on your canvas. Mix the paint up; don't worry about getting multiple colors on your brush. Use gel medium to thin the paint.

3 *Paper.*

Use gel medium or white glue to apply torn scraps of text, pretty, decorative paper and/or antique paper randomly. Use a paper towel to wipe the excess gel medium off so that the text does not wrinkle. If you're not quite ready for paper yet, throw that task back into the bowl and draw another. But why not just give it a whirl; a bit of magic might just be on your side, after all.

4 *Ink.*

Dribble, brush, spill, splash, scribble or wipe fountain pen ink willy-nilly. Close your eyes when you do it so you aren't too precise. Use different colors of ink, should you so desire.

5 *Chalk/Pastels.*

Use oil pastels or chalks randomly to color areas or create lines and shapes. Be flagrant, messy, rough. If you break the chalk (my . . .you must have been working out!) more power to you!

7 *Charcoal.*

Create depth by sketching, outlining, drawing or shading with a charcoal pencil. I like to rub it on the edges of torn paper. Sadly, areas covered with gel medium will not accept the charcoal easily. Hey, just sand them first!

6 *Photograph.*

Select a photograph from your private collection (sounds so fancy-pants, doesn't it?), vintage or new. Here, I've taped a framed, vintage tintype to the collage. It can be glued, attached with brads, stapled, or all of the above. The photograph can be whole or torn—maybe even cut with decorative scissors. Maybe it is a compilation of several photographs cut and spliced together.

8 *Smudge.*

Wet your fingers and wipe your artwork to create smudges. This works especially well with charcoal pencil, but can also work with wet paint, non-water-resistant ink, or chalks and pastels. No finger double-dipping, please.

9 *Magazine*.

Tear a page (or portion thereof) from a magazine. The cheaper the magazine, the better. Black and white photos from fashion magazines work great, as does large letter text. Use gel medium or glue to adhere it to your collage and wipe the excess gel medium from it so that it will lie flat. WIPE. Use wet baby wipes to wipe away (remove) areas of paint and ink. The more you rub a magazine, the more ink comes off, and the more distressed it appears. This technique also removes excess paint, pastels, chalk, charcoal and more. Baby wipes—not just for babies anymore!

10 *Stamp*.

Choose any rubber stamp and any color ink and stamp once, twice, thrice . . . you decide. I prefer water-resistant ink like StazOn. But smudged or stamped images that have run can create wonderful effects. Go with what you have and accept it.

11 *Pattern*.

Create a pattern with any medium. Here, I used paint to create a line of polka dots. A pattern can be a series of rubber stamps, lines drawn in a row with charcoal pencil, letters cut from old books and glued down. Webster says a pattern is a consistent, characteristic form, style or method. I just consider a pattern one thing repeated at least three times.

12 *Draw*.

No! You do not need to *draw* a new slip! (Different kind of *draw*!) Use pencil, pen or ink to outline something already on your collage. Or draw a new shape, such as a house. The drawing can be an intricate sketch or a simple line drawing. You will not be graded on this step, I promise!

13 Sand.

Sand the surface in various spots to remove layers. Select the grade of sandpaper you wish to use. Allow the texture of the grit to show through. Make sure to sand when the paint is dry (or not) and wipe off the dust. Sand the photograph, too. Please, do not plug in your belt sander; you will not work up a sweat doing this.

14 Scratch.

Scratch your artwork using an awl, craft knife, scissors or other sharp object. You may scratch randomly, or scratch a pattern in the surface. Do not leave sharp objects within reach of children or cats.

15 Text.

When you select the prompt that says "text" get excited! This is my favorite task, and a great creative challenge! Tear one (and only one) page from an old book. You will do three things with this page:

1. Cut out the page number and use it somewhere in the collage. (Perhaps this is your lucky lottery number? Perhaps this is how many traffic tickets you are going to get in your lifetime?)
2. Use a sentence with at least three consecutive words from anywhere in the text. (The sentence should appear in your collage exactly as it is taken from the book, but you may add text before or after the sentence.)
3. Create a new sentence using individual words that you cut from the page and rearrange. (Run-on sentences are acceptable as are those that do not contain verbs, adjectives, conjunctions or punctuation.)

You will not be graded on this task either, but extra points are awarded for creativity. You will be amazed at the magic that blossoms when you perform this task. Use white glue or gel medium to apply the text to your collage.

16 Write.

Write anything (a word or phrase or single letter), any size (small or large), with pencil, pen, ink, crayon, blunt object or other writing utensil. Use poor penmanship. Misspell. Choose what you want to write by opening the telephone book and pointing. Write backwards. Write with your left hand. Write in a foreign language. Write wrong.

17 3-D.

If you draw this slip, you are going to add dimensional objects (thicker than a piece of paper) such as pressed flowers, ribbon, beads, game pieces, and so on to your collage. Let your imagination run wild. Nothing is off limits (including your husband's prize coin). OK. Maybe *that* is off limits. Attach the objects to your collage with adhesive caulk.

18 Surprise.

This is a freebie! You choose the task. It can be something you've already done or something you have never done. Ever! Surprise yourself. Search your kitchen cabinets for options. Or your underwear drawer! The sky is the limit. When you've run out of tasks to pull out of the bowl, or you must leave to pick up the kids after school, the last, but NOT LEAST, thing to do is sign your name! I did it here, using "SALLY" cut from an old book, and writing "JEAN" with charcoal pencil. You never know. Someday your children's children may be able to sell it to pay for a week at Harvard.

Collage Cargo

The majority of projects in this book will require a bit of collage work as a starting point. As I hope I have just shown you, there are no rules for making beautiful collage creations. Use what inspires you, and you will make magic. Here are a few things that I recommend you keep within reach when the muse strikes, but feel free to add any of your own secret ingredients!

surface to create on (cardstock, watercolor paper; canvas—whatever you're comfortable with)

vintage papers (old books [don't leave out dime-store novels!], antique postcards, old ledger paper, love letters and so on)

vintage or personal photos

acrylic paints (your favorite colors as well as some you've been wanting to experiment with) and brushes, of course

gel medium, white glue, Diamond Glaze (Judikins) and clear caulk (for adhering collage elements as well as sealing)

chalk, pastels, crayons and charcoal (my charcoal pencil is one of my favorite supplies)

pencil

rubber stamps and inkpads

pretty papers that you love (wallpaper; scrapbook paper; doilies, wrapping paper; tissue paper; handmade paper—whatever brings a smile)

sandpaper or sanding block

craft knife and scissors (these are both good to scratch with as well)

heat gun (for the impatient)

glitter (German glass glitter has magical powers)

fountain pen and ink

three-dimensional goodies (buttons, crumpled chocolate wrappers, charms, beads, shells, trinkets, coins, small toys)

Glass-Cutting Greatness

Now that the secret is out and you are pulling beautiful collages out of a hat night and day, the time has come for you to cut the glass that will protect your lovelies and allow you to sport them wherever you may roam. Cutting glass is not as scary as it sounds. Just remember to always wear your safety glasses. Très-chic!

STRAIGHT CUTS

This is as easy as 1-2-3, and your first project will be a snap!
All that's needed is a straight edge and a handheld cutter.

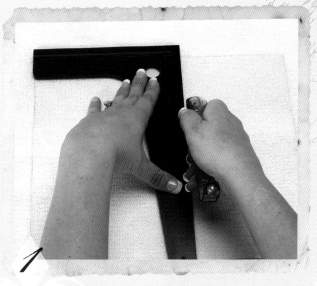

Align your straight edge next to the mark you want to cut on and apply moderate pressure with the cutter as you slide along the straight edge to score the glass.

Position the "snapper" pliers so that the line on the pliers is centered with the score line on the glass.

Squeeze the pliers to snap the glass and break it.

CIRCULAR CUTS

While some prefer going down the straight and narrow, sometimes a girl wants a few curves!
While this type of cutting may take just a bit more practice, once you learn to add circles and
other curves, the possibilities are endless.

1

Set your circular cutter to the diameter
you wish to cut. Slide a piece of glass
under the wheel and apply pressure to
the cutter as you go around in a circle
to score the glass.

2

To free the circle from the center of
the piece of glass, first make straight
cuts from the circle outward to the
edge of the glass, like sun rays.

3

Use glass nips to grip the scored pieces
and break them off individually.

SHAPING WITH SPECIALTY CUTTERS

These three tools will add panache to your basic glass shapes by dulling the sharp edges and
making them more inviting. (This also ensures long life for those cute little digits.)

GLASS GRINDER

A grinder can be used to simply round
corners on a rectangle or dull a sharp
edge. It can also be used to remove
larger areas of glass, like when you want
to turn a rectangle into an oval. Be sure
your grinder is full of water and set up
properly according to the manufacturer's instructions.

GLASS HAND FILE

Slide the corner, or edge of the glass
down the stone. Then rotate it slightly
and slide it back up. Keep the stone or
file wet to avoid excess shards. This is
similar to filing your nails, and great if
you are reluctant to use a power tool.

GLASS RING SAW

This tool cuts through glass like butter!
It can be used to slice through bottles,
cut stems off wine glasses, or to cut an
unusual shape out of flat glass. Simply
push the glass through the blade.

Sublime Solder Secrets

Soldering your pretty little pieces is the final step and the one that really shines! There are many brands and types of solder available, but nothing less than true silver satisfies this fussy girl. Practice your soldering style on the following three quickie-projects and by the time I teach you to clean and polish your work, you'll be ready to jump into any project in the book. Just don't forget your suitcase!

Unpacking Your Soldering Suitcase

With the exception of the project on page 54, all of the pretty little things in this book will require basic soldering supplies. While you may not need every item for every project, by stocking your suitcase well, you'll never be caught unprepared. Follow the setup I've shown you here, and success is sure to be yours each and every time!

glass-cutting supplies

> safety glasses
>
> straight edge and cutting mat
>
> permanent marker
>
> handheld cutter
> (one with a pivoting head is nice)
>
> breaker/grozer pliers
>
> running pliers or nips
>
> grinder (preferred) or
> handheld glass file
>
> ring saw for glass (optional)

copper tape

> ¼", ⅜", ½" (6mm, 10mm, 13mm)
> (for most projects, I prefer black-backed)

slug barrier tape (hardware stores)
or adhesive-backed sheet
(stained-glass stores or online suppliers)

bone folder

flux (the gel type is great because it doesn't drip)

flux brush

solder (you can use what you like, but I will not use anything other than Silvergleem by Canfield—it really shines!)

soldering iron (you will need one hot enough to melt the type of solder you decide to use—one with a thermostat is best)

iron stand (with a place for a wet sponge)

third hand jewelry tool (Who doesn't need this?)

metal blocks (for stablity as you solder)

flux and patina remover/cleaner

metal polish cream, toothbrush and cloth for buffing

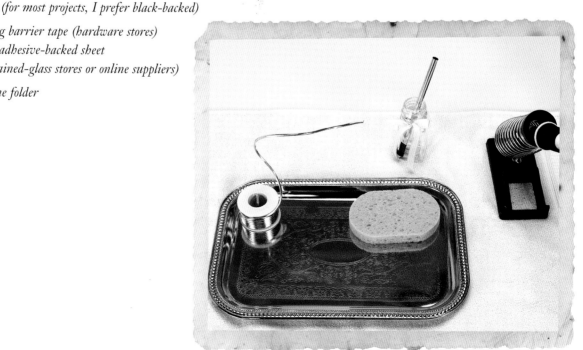

SOLDERING A SINGLE SURFACE

When you have a large surface to cover with solder, such as the back of this single bubble, cutting pieces of copper barrier tape is an easy way to give your soldering a seamless look.

1

Print artwork onto matte paper in a water-resistant ink, or use original images, such as from a book. Coat the back of a glass nugget with Diamond Glaze, and then press it onto the paper. After the glaze has dried, use scissors to trim the excess paper around the nugget.

2

Wrap the nugget with tape (begin at the edge near the back of the nugget.) Roll the tape around the nugget.

3

Fold the excess tape over to the back and burnish.

4

Trace the nugget onto a piece of copper slug barrier tape and then cut the circle out, slightly smaller than the shape.

5.

Peel the backing off of the tape and adhere the circle to the back of the nugget. The bubble is not quite ready to solder.

Sally's Top Five Soldering Secrets

{1} Flux is your friend. If the solder isn't flowing nicely for you, just add a touch of flux to the solder, to the tip, or to the piece.

{2} Don't overwork your pieces. Sometimes the fix is worse than the original problem. Move along.

{3} Let the soldering iron tip work for you. Before moving the solder along, let the tip melt it first. The tip makes the magic happen.

{4} Practice, practice, practice. Each time you solder, it will be better than the last. Save your first pieces, then down the road, have yourself a little "trunk show" showing "before" and "after."

{5} Congratulate yourself. Give yourself credit. Be proud that you've picked up a hot tool and took it upon yourself to make something beautiful.

6

Brush flux over all the copper. While the bubble is lying on the work surface, cover the entire back of it with solder, picking up only a little bit of solder at a time. Then, solder the sides.

TAPING AND SOLDERING AROUND AN ATTACHMENT

Copper tape is good at hiding things, like the transition from glass to a thumbtack. Burnish the tape on the tack as dutifully as you have learned to on the glass.

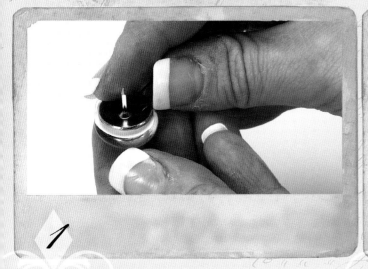

1

To make a bubble into a thumbtack, use caulk to adhere the nugget to the flat side of a thumbtack. Let dry.

2

Position the tape so that most of the overhang is on the back.

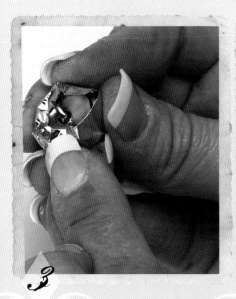

3

Press the tape around onto the tack and burnish all the way around.

4

Cover all of the copper with flux, using a flux brush.

5

Touch the tip of the hot iron to the solder coil to pick up some solder. Apply the solder on the tip of the iron to the copper tape to transfer it. Continue picking up small amounts of solder and covering the tape until it is completely covered.

TAPING OVER A SEAM BETWEEN TWO PIECES

Sometimes you will want to glue two pieces of glass back-to-back. In the case of these bubbles, that leaves a crevice. Copper tape will hide this gap and make the transition seamless.

1

Prepare two nuggets that are the same size, with their images (see step 1, page 23). On the back of each nugget, mark the top with a dot using a permanent marker.

2

Apply a dollop of clear caulk to the back of one nugget.

3

Press the backs of the two nuggets together, matching up their dots at the top.

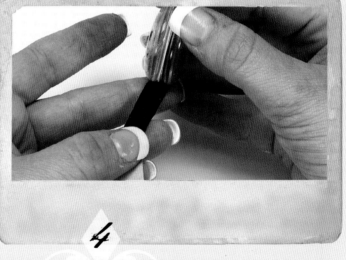

4

Trim a length of black-backed copper tape to go around the perimeter of the nugget sandwich. Peel off the first portion of the backing paper and center the bubble over the width of the tape.

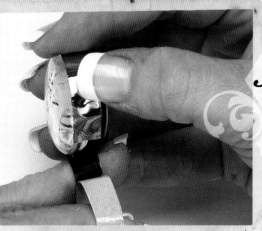

5

Wrap the tape around the sandwich.

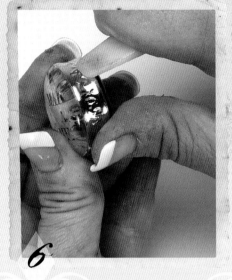

6

Burnish the tape onto the glass on both edges of the tape.

7

Apply flux to the tape around the "double bubble." Begin soldering at the seam area, propping the nuggets up between the nose of a pliers. After the section has set, rotate the bubble to continue soldering.

8

To attach a jump ring at the seam area, when you have completed the soldering, grip the ring in needle-nose pliers. Hold it so that the open end is exposed and brush some flux on it. Pick up a bit of solder on the tip of the iron and, while holding the jump ring to the seam on the bubble, apply the solder to the ring and bubble. Hold it while the solder sets. After it has cooled, put a bit more solder on top of the ring.

MAKING YOUR WORK SPARKLE

When you're done soldering, you will want to clean and polish your pieces. If you decide to use silver solder, your pieces will tarnish over time, but you can always shine them up, just like when your mother asked you to polish the holiday silverware.

Apply flux cleaner.

Use a soft cloth and some flux and patina remover to gently clean the flux off the finished piece. This is better than using water, which can seep under the tape and solder, and potentially ruin your artwork.

Adding shine.

The piece can then be polished with metal polish cream, using a toothbrush or a cloth. Squeeze some polish onto the cloth, then rub it onto the solder. Next, use a clean part of the cloth to buff it off. Lovely!

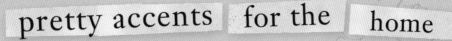

pretty accents for the home

It is often a lack of beauty that makes things beautiful. Torn and stained paper, a chipped domino doll head, a missing button . . . It's like the ugly duckling turning into a swan. I like the ugly duckling just the way he is. To me, that IS beauty.

Each year, I sought out the biggest, fattest, fullest, tallest Christmas tree. I wanted the showpiece. One year, Brad, my husband, brought home a tree. It was narrow, had bare spots, and when he trimmed the trunk he cut it too short. Well, out went that tree! The next day I found myself traumatized. I felt as if I had hurt the tree's feelings—that I had rained on nature's parade. Oh, how I regretted getting rid of the imperfect tree. Ever since then, at holiday time, I search for the homeliest Christmas tree I can find, and give it a good home. I see the beauty in the bare spots, the crooked shape; I love it just the way it is.

Well-worn objects have a sense of history. Blocks that were played with by children. Innermost thoughts scribbled in diaries in pencil, smudged and water-soaked after being tucked away for 100+ years. Somebody once loved the now-broken teapot, but discarded it when it was no longer perfect. Now, I love it. Sometimes I think inanimate objects have feelings. They say that one person's trash is anothers treasure, but it goes beyond that for me. An old boyfriend said that I was a diamond in the rough. But the man I married thinks I am a diamond now—maybe "cloudy," maybe "mis-chiselled," but a diamond "as-is," just the same. In fact, I love the terms "as-is" and "fixer-upper."

So I take the unwanted, well-used, broken fragments of the past and give them new life. No longer are Grandmother's pearls piled in a box in the back of a drawer. Now they swim with their long lost "pearl" relatives, some adorned by long-since-read words, amongst other neglected and unwanted treasures. Others will love them now, give them a new home and cherish them.

Welcome these castaways into your home. You'll see that they are indeed beautiful. Give them a good home. Cherish them. Love them and they may just love you back!

Write what you like; there is no other rule.

O. Henry

FLOWER-POWER Pen

I'VE TRIED FRESH FLOWERS IN VASES. I've tried and failed. The next day, the flowers are face-down, sorrowful little creatures. But a jar full of flower *pens* can survive without water. Without those little packets of plant food. Without "sweet-talk." All they need is a little "writing" nourishment now and again. Give flower pens as a special gift to your friends. The Flower-Power Pen even makes bill-paying sweeter! You'll find yourself giving up e-mail in order to write more letters to your pen pals!

ingredients

collage cargo (see page 19)

soldering suitcase (see page 22)

½" (13mm) diameter acrylic or glass tubing

disposable pen such as a BIC

hacksaw for cutting acrylic or ring saw
for cutting glass

needle-nose pliers

faux flower with at least
a ⅜" (10mm) stem

epoxy

Want more?

Personalize the pen by adding a name, initial, or special message such as "Happy Birthday" to the collage work inside of the tube or on the collaged petals.

1

Using a hacksaw (for acrylic) or glass ring saw (see page 21), cut the acrylic or glass tube to a 6" (15cm) length (or long enough so that when the pen is in the tube, with the writing tip fully outside of the tube, the opposite end of the pen is recessed ⅜" [10cm] from the tube's other end). Create a collage piece that is about 6" × 1½" (15cm × 4cm) and make a color photocopy of it (or use it as-is, if it is pliable enough to roll easily). Trim the copy or excess collage paper to the above size and roll it around the pen.

2

Feed the rolled artwork and pen into the tube. (The artwork will expand to fit the tube so you do not need to glue it in place.)

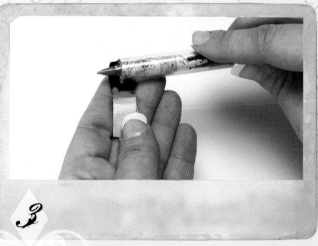

3

Line up the tip of the pen with the edge of the tube (as shown). Apply copper tape to the tube and wrap it around making sure to overlap it on itself by about ¼" (6mm).

4

Gently fold the copper tape toward the pen tip, hold the tip in a pair of needle-nose pliers, and burnish. (Be careful not to push the pen tip back into the tube.)

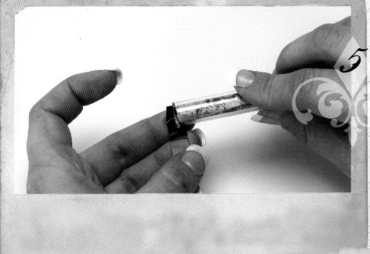

Apply ¼" (6mm) copper tape to the blunt end of the tube. Fold this over and into the interior of the tube. Burnish smooth.

Beginning with the pen tip, solder the copper-taped areas of the tube (see page 23). If you are using acrylic tubing, it can potentially melt when it gets too hot (which would not be a good thing), so apply the solder in small amounts and quickly pull back on the iron. Press the pen against a wet sponge to cool it before applying more solder. Cool the tip of the soldering iron on the wet sponge as well. Be patient with this step.

6

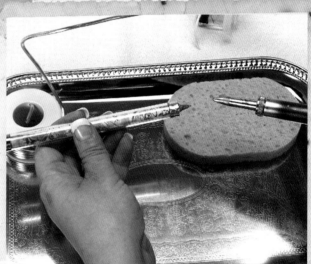

7

Carefully solder the blunt end of the tube following the instructions in the last step. Begin soldering around the inside of the tube, then the edge, then the outside. Cool the soldering iron and the pen on the wet sponge often. Clean and polish.

8 Take the faux flower head and paint it or collage it with vintage, handwritten text. Write words. Use rubber stamps. Number each petal . . . you know, embellish it here and there, and let dry. Use your fingers to apply adhesive caulk to the edges of a few petals. Dip the flower in glitter and shake off the excess. Let dry. Here I've used German glass glitter, which will tarnish beautifully as it ages. Continue adding glitter as you desire. Don't forget the stamen!

9 Squeeze epoxy into the blunt end of the tube. Stick the stem into the tube and the epoxy. (This is why the pen is recessed from the edge of the tube.) Prop the tube upright and let the adhesive cure.

PEN BOUQUET

Inspiration comes so much easier when you sit down to a cup containing your own personal flower-pen bouquet. Whether you're writing a love note, a thank-you card or even being forced to sit through bill-paying time, the only thing that will make writing a challenge now will be choosing which pen to use!

If you wish to know the divine, feel the wind on your face and the warm sun on your back.

Eido Tai Shimano Roshi

PRETTY
Paperweight

THERE I WAS. Windows open and the freshness of spring spilling into my living room. Soft breezes carrying the fragrance of newly blooming daffodils swirling about. Here and there, the chirp of a bird, hungry for my daily offering of peanuts. The sun, streaming through the swaying, leaf-covered branches, cast a golden sheen across the room. Oh, the pleasure of a warm, spring day.... All of a sudden, a gust of wind barreled through the window, leaving curtains flapping in its wake—so strong that it caused teacups to chatter, candles to go dark, tables to suddenly be "dusted." I glanced in fear at my desk, where I had just methodically sorted bills, letters and love notes. (OK—there were no love notes. Hmph!) To my surprise (and delight) not a single paper was out of place. But, of course! My bills and letters were tucked neatly beneath my Pretty Paperweight. Today was my lucky day! Everything was in order and my house was magically dusted as a bonus—hooray!

ingredients

collage cargo (see page 19)

soldering suitcase (see page 22)

blank round paperweight
(a new paperweight, a vintage
paperweight with the artwork removed,
or a thick lens)

square of felt
(for the paperweight's underside)

epoxy

Want more?

Create intricate artwork on a large scale. Photograph the artwork or scan it and reduce it on your computer. Reduce it to the size of your paperweight and print it out on matte photo paper with waterproof inks. When it is behind the glass of the paperweight, it takes on a new life and the details of the intricate artwork really shine.

1

Using the paperweight as a template, cut your original, or scanned and printed artwork, to fit. Apply Diamond Glaze directly to the back of the paperweight, and press your artwork, face down, into the adhesive. Burnish it well to work out any bubbles. Let it dry and apply several additional coats of Diamond Glaze to the back of the artwork, allowing each coat to dry between applications. Wrap copper tape around the base of the paperweight, placing half of the tape on the rim and etting the other half extend as excess. Overlap the seam as usual (about ¼" [6mm]). Fold the excess toward the bottom of the paperweight. Burnish the tape smooth. Apply flux and solder to the outside edge of the paperweight first. Here, I've risked life and limb by holding the paperweight directly in my hands. Every once in awhile hot, molten solder will drop on my fingers and, well, it hurts. To avoid this, prop the paperweight between metal blocks, hold it with pliers, or cover your hand with a towel.

2

Next, solder all the copper-taped areas on the bottom.

3

To make cute, little dots around the edge of the base, prop the paperweight on its side. Hold the solder with one hand allowing for a "tail" of solder to extend and touch the soldered edge of the paperweight. Use your other hand to hold the soldering iron. Touch the iron to the solder and melt it until a drop of solder rolls off and attaches itself to the edge of the paperweight. Then, lift your soldering iron off. (This may take a bit of practice.) Continue all the way around the paperweight, making cute little dots wherever your little heart desires.

4

Clean and polish the soldered areas. Trim felt to approximately ⅛" (3mm) smaller than the circumference of the bottom of your paperweight. Spread epoxy over the paperweight's bottom, and press the paperweight onto the felt. Rub your hand over the felt, making sure to get a secure connection. Here, I've used neutral black. Ta da! You've done it!

Don't buy the house, buy the neighborhood.

Russian Proverb

Neighborhood

I'VE LONG THOUGHT OF MY HOUSE as a place to display pretty things, to have in order, to decorate "just so." But, when I decided to leave my day job in search of the simple life where family comes first, where dust bunnies are pretend pets, where "house" means *home*, everything changed. It brings tears to my eyes to think of the years I overlooked what is most important. So, when I thought about making a neighborhood, a series of houses (aka "homes"), what I thought of first was my family—my three children. With this in mind, I scavenged for three cabinet cards that represented each of my children and personalized the collaging of them. For instance, on the front of each I put my children's birthdates which are actually page numbers cut from vintage books. On the back is an old anagram game piece representing their first initial (all Es) and more text taken from old books. The completed "neighborhood," now displayed front and center on my mantle, is my favorite piece of artwork. And when visitors stop by and are surrounded by toys and textbooks and dust bunnies—oh, my! I point to my neighborhood and they understand completely.

ingredients

collage cargo (see page 19)

soldering suitcase (see page 22)

house-shaped, beveled glass, 6 pieces (available at many stained-glass stores) approximately 4" × 6" (10cm × 15cm)

jump rings (8mm or 9mm), 12

10" (25cm) lengths of 16-gauge, tinned copper wire, 2

wire cutters

round-nose pliers

1

Using one piece of beveled glass as a template, cut three cabinet cards or vintage photos to the shape of the glass, then collage and embellish the three pieces, front and back. Clean the glass, and sandwich each piece of artwork between two pieces, making sure that the beveled sides of the glass are on the outside. Holding the glass firmly between your fingers, wrap each piece with ½" (13cm) copper tape positioning the seam at the bottom. Fold the edges over at 90-degree angles and burnish smooth. Solder the copper-taped areas for each of the three houses. Clean and polish.

2

Lay the three house shapes down in the order that you want. Solder three jump rings to each side of the center shape (they should be evenly spaced beginning about ¼" [6mm] from the top and ½" [13mm] from the bottom.) There should be a total of six jump rings (three on each side) on the center shape.

3

Solder three jump rings to the inside sides of the other two houses, making sure to stagger the jump rings just a bit, so as not to interfere with the placement of the center shape's rings. When you are finished, you will have a total of twelve jump rings as shown.

4

Align the three shapes together. Feed a piece of wire through the jump rings of the center and one adjoining side shape, to hinge them together. Use round-nosed pliers to twirl the bottom excess into a small spiral. Do the same for the top excess but with a much larger spiral. For fun, dangle a bead from the swirl. Repeat for the other side.

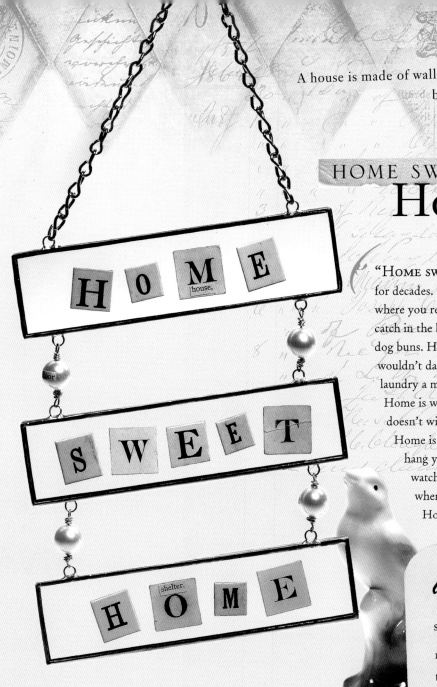

A house is made of walls and beams;
but a home is built with love and dreams.

Author Unknown

HOME SWEET
Home

"HOME SWEET HOME." A sentiment that has been around for decades. But never before has it meant so much. Home is where you relax after a hard day's work. Home is where you play catch in the backyard. Home is where the barbeque burns the hot dog buns. Home is where you cry while watching tearjerkers you wouldn't dare watch at a theatre. Home is where you pile the laundry a mile high and promise yourself you'll do it tomorrow. Home is where you watch the dog chase the cat and hope he doesn't win. Home is where you celebrate the little victories. Home is where you overcome defeats. Home is where you hang your pictures and your heart. Home is where you watch the sunrise welcome a brand new day. Home is where you kiss your children good night.
Home Sweet Home.

ingredients

soldering suitcase (see page 22)

1/16" (2mm) window glass cut to 2" × 6" (5cm × 15cm), 6

vintage anagram game pieces (the thin cardboard kind) or paper squares with letters printed on them

white glue

Diamond Glaze with brush

jump rings (8mm or 9mm), 10

20-gauge wire (tinned copper or sterling silver)

wire cutters

large beads or pearls, 4

link chain, 8" (20cm)

Want more?

This is a great way to showcase a special bit of ephemera. Perhaps a vintage concert ticket, centered within glass, can become an amazing pendant. Postage stamps from places you have been can be a wonderful background to rubber stamps which spell "travel." Hang this vertically with a crystal dangling from the bottom. Sometimes, the smallest item, surrounded by a large expanse of clear glass, can create quite a dramatic effect. Ooh la la.

1

Grind down the edges of the glass slightly. Embellish the anagrams with found words and antique paper. For example, glue a snippet of vintage paper to the back of each anagram letter. Then, for a chosen few, glue a single word, a date or a teeny-tiny photo, to the front of the anagram. Use white glue to adhere the embellishments.

3

2

Clean the glass and arrange the letters on the glass as you desire. Use a dab of Diamond Glaze on the back of each letter to secure it to the glass. Let dry.

Place a second piece of glass on top and wrap with copper tape. Make sure the seam is on the top, about ½" (13mm) from the corner. Solder the copper-taped areas completely. Solder two jump rings to the top and bottom, about ½" (13mm) in from the corners, of the top two shapes. Solder jump rings to the top only of the bottom shape. Clean and polish. Create a loop of wire and put it through the bottom jump ring of the top piece. Wrap the wire around and around and snip of any excess. Thread a bead or pearl onto the remaining wire, then create another loop that will go through the top jump ring of the next shape. Wrap the wire around and snip off any excess. Do this for all four connections. Oh, by the way, sloppy wire wrapping is good— it indicates that your artwork was created by hand.

4

Open the end link of the chain and secure it to the jump ring of the top shape. Secure the other end of the chain to the opposite jump ring.

A Little More:
MEMORY-GO-ROUND

Sometimes it isn't what you see, but
what you see beyond what is already there.
It is easy to see through something transparent. But, if you try hard enough, you can even
see through that which is opaque.

Your eyes stop at the first roadblock and
consider it. Then, they move through it,
because you allow them to look beyond. When
your vision takes you there (beyond), it opens
up possibilities. Infinite possibilities. Is that
a wall behind the glass? What was on the
wall before? What colors of paint are below?
What color? Why was it that color?

And the timbers behind the wall—
who put them there? Who built the home?
What were they thinking as they held up that
beam? Before the house was there, was it a
field? Did children play there? What did they
play? Did they laugh? How did they feel when
their field was replaced with the house?
Next time you look at something, look
through it. Look beyond it. Let your mind
take you somewhere. Somewhere else.

ingredients

soldering suitcase (see page 22)

oval, beveled glass 3" × 5"
(8cm × 13cm), 2 pieces

jump rings, 7mm, 2

link chain, 7" (18cm)

scrap of fabric
(that is meaningful to you)

safety pin, hat pin, or other attachment

snippet of text (relating to the theme)

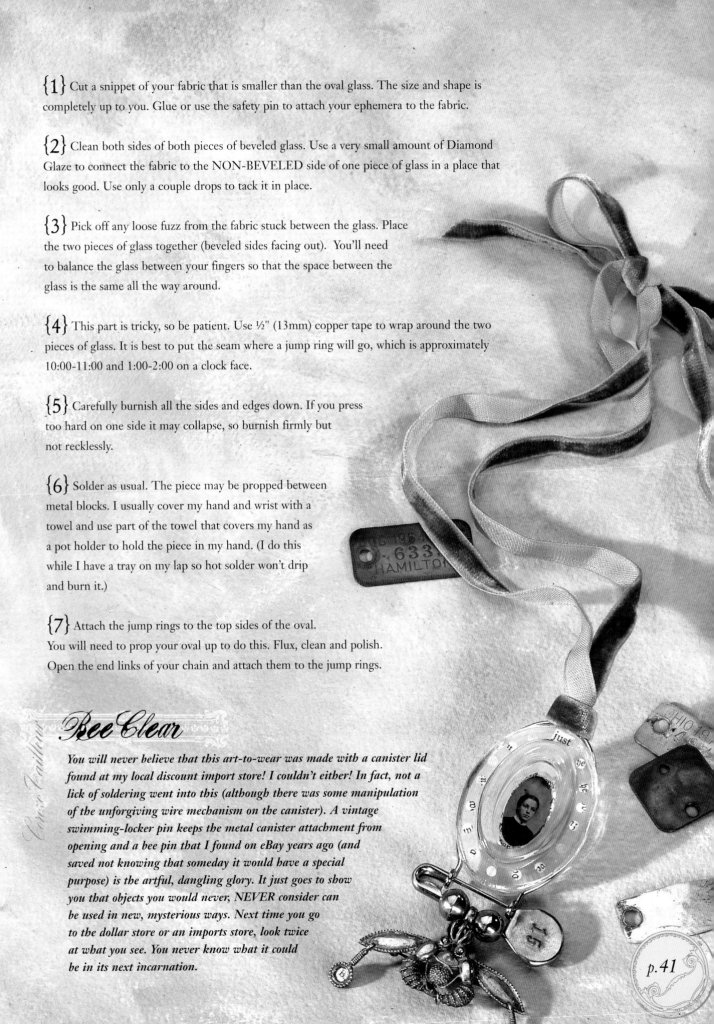

{1} Cut a snippet of your fabric that is smaller than the oval glass. The size and shape is completely up to you. Glue or use the safety pin to attach your ephemera to the fabric.

{2} Clean both sides of both pieces of beveled glass. Use a very small amount of Diamond Glaze to connect the fabric to the NON-BEVELED side of one piece of glass in a place that looks good. Use only a couple drops to tack it in place.

{3} Pick off any loose fuzz from the fabric stuck between the glass. Place the two pieces of glass together (beveled sides facing out). You'll need to balance the glass between your fingers so that the space between the glass is the same all the way around.

{4} This part is tricky, so be patient. Use ½" (13mm) copper tape to wrap around the two pieces of glass. It is best to put the seam where a jump ring will go, which is approximately 10:00-11:00 and 1:00-2:00 on a clock face.

{5} Carefully burnish all the sides and edges down. If you press too hard on one side it may collapse, so burnish firmly but not recklessly.

{6} Solder as usual. The piece may be propped between metal blocks. I usually cover my hand and wrist with a towel and use part of the towel that covers my hand as a pot holder to hold the piece in my hand. (I do this while I have a tray on my lap so hot solder won't drip and burn it.)

{7} Attach the jump rings to the top sides of the oval. You will need to prop your oval up to do this. Flux, clean and polish. Open the end links of your chain and attach them to the jump rings.

Bee Clear

You will never believe that this art-to-wear was made with a canister lid found at my local discount import store! I couldn't either! In fact, not a lick of soldering went into this (although there was some manipulation of the unforgiving wire mechanism on the canister). A vintage swimming-locker pin keeps the metal canister attachment from opening and a bee pin that I found on eBay years ago (and saved not knowing that someday it would have a special purpose) is the artful, dangling glory. It just goes to show you that objects you would never, NEVER consider can be used in new, mysterious ways. Next time you go to the dollar store or an imports store, look twice at what you see. You never know what it could be in its next incarnation.

A house is no home   unless it contains food and fire   for the mind as well as the body.

Margaret Fuller

"LIGHT" House

ONE IF BY LAND, TWO IF BY SEA. This house is so pretty, you'll want to make three! Fashion yourself a bevy of beacons throughout your home. Soon, you'll be making these for friends and family (no doubt you'll find yourself with more friends than you can imagine). Your electric bill will skyrocket, you won't have any outlets left for the TV, but that's okay—your life will be luminous.

ingredients

collage cargo (see page 19)

soldering suitcase (see page 22)

house-shaped, beveled glass, 2

$1/16$" (2mm) window glass, cut to match the shape of the house-shaped glass, 2

$1/16$" window glass, cut to 5" × 3¾" (13cm × 10cm), 4

$1/16$" (2mm) window glass, cut to 4" × 3¾" (10cm × 10cm), 4

masking or duct tape

1" × 6" (3cm × 15cm) piece of pine or fir approximately 2' (61cm) long

drill with bit large enough to create a hole for the light-assembly tube

wood glue

light assembly (including cord, plug, electrical components, bulb [usually sold separately])

Create artwork that includes silhouettes for a dramatic effect. Also, white-on-white letters that spell words or names become beautiful imagery when illuminated. To do this, make sure that the white background is semi-transparent and the white letters are clear and opaque.

1

Gently grind the corners of all twelve pieces of glass. Create artwork for the house using the glass pieces as templates. Keep in mind that the artwork should not be too dense as the light is supposed to illuminate its details from inside. Clean the glass and sandwich the artwork between each piece of glass. Wrap them in copper tape, making sure that the seams for all four sides of the house are at the bottom, and the seams for both sides of the roof are at the top. Burnish smooth. Solder all six sections individually. Clean and polish. Prop one house-shaped section and one wide side at a 90-degree angle. Use metal blocks or other heavy items to prop. Tack solder these together on the outside seam. Then, lay one side down flat and solder along the inside seam.

2

Flip the house over again and finish soldering the outside seam smoothly.

3

Repeat the soldering process for the other two sides of the house. Pay attention to the sides you're putting together. It's important to solder the rectangular sides placed behind the house-shape, instead of next to the house-shape, at the edge. Place both 2-piece sections together and tack solder them on the outside first, then on the inside, and then a final smooth soldering on the outside. Clean the flux off.

4

Use masking tape or duct tape to secure both sides of the roof to the top of the lighthouse. The sections should meet directly in the center over the peak of the house so that it leaves an equal valley between the two sections. Apply drops of solder beginning at the center, moving to the edges and then between the centers and the edges. I prefer the visual appearance of the drops of solder every 3/8" (10mm) or so. However, you may continue adding solder to create a smooth finish in the valley of the roof. Clean and polish the house.

5

Cut 1" (3cm) fir or pine to the following dimensions: 6" × 5¾" (15cm × 15cm) and 3¾" × 3½" (10cm × 9cm). Drill a hole in the center that is wide enough to fit the light assembly snugly, but not so large that it is loose. The light assembly usually comes with a cardboard tube. Test the assembly to make sure it fits.

Paint and collage the visible surfaces of the wood base to coordinate with the artwork of the house. Coat it with gel medium to protect it. Allow to dry. Center the two wood pieces on top of each other and glue them in place. Let dry. Attach feet to the bottom of the house base using adhesive glue. Options include square alphabet blocks, glass cabinet knobs, game pieces—have fun with this step.

Assemble the electrical components, gluing the cardboard tube to the base if it is loose, and inserting a low-wattage bulb (follow the light assembly instructions). Place the house on the base and flip the switch. *Voila!*

6

TINY NEIGHBORHOOD

It's no fun living in the middle of nowhere with no one around to borrow sugar from! Here's a little neighborhood of your very own—little pink houses (or whatever color your heart desires). They come in all shapes and sizes (as most neighbors do), and are lit from inside with tea lights. If you pay attention to the glow they cast, you can imagine the homes filled with family enjoying a nice, crackling fire and sharing stories from their days. This is what makes a house a home and a neighborhood a place to be.

Flowers are the sweetest things

God ever made and forgot to put a soul into.

Henry Ward Beecher

Bud Vase

WE ALL HAVE THEM: A stash of vases tucked deep within the recesses of our kitchen cabinets, high upon shelves in our garage, under the stairs to the basement. Empty. Dusty. Just waiting for a nice (or apologetic) husband to bring us flowers. Well, we all know the chances of *that* happening! But what if we had hanging vases nestled in swirls of silver with tassels and fringe? A single flower is all this sassy flower-holder needs! Surely a hubby can spring for a $1.50 bud at the supermarket! But if not, skip the flower and opt for a candle instead. Or pencils. Or pixie sticks. Or eyeliner pencils. Nearly anything would look marvelous tucked inside this decorative vase.

ingredients

soldering suitcase (see page 22)

champagne or wine glass

paper text snippets

Diamond Glaze and brush

beaded fringe on a ribbon
(slightly longer than the length of
the circumference of the glass rim)

alligator clips or clothespins, 2 or 3

16-gauge tinned copper wire, 18"–20"
(46cm–51cm)

wire cutters

round-nose pliers

elements for the tassel (such as a
vintage fabric tape measure, glass
dowel [used for glass bead making],
grosgrain ribbon, string of beads,
crystals, charms, old keys or tags)

jump rings (7mm), several

Want more?

The vase can hold so many things besides flowers: pencils, tea lights, hair sticks, swizzle sticks, barbeque skewers, rubber bands, paper clips, candy, a small plant . . .

1

Cut the stem off a wine or champagne glass with a ring saw or score it by hand and snap it off. Grind the edge smooth.

2

Clean the glass inside and out. Use Diamond Glaze to collage elements to the inside of the glass. Decorative tissue, letters from days gone by and words cut from old books for instance. Thinner papers work best. Seal the images with multiple coats (at least five) of Diamond Glaze to keep the elements waterproof. Clean the glass again. Lay out the beaded trim, and position a length of copper tape so that half of it runs along the ribbon, and the other half overhangs as excess. Fold over the remaining half. Flux and solder this, being careful not to melt the threads or the beads.

3

Apply half the width of a length of copper tape to the top rim of the glass. Fold it over and burnish smooth. Apply copper tape to the stub end of the glass (where the stem was cut off). Solder both areas. Solder a jump ring to the center of the stub. Prop the wine glass upright. (Here, I used three metal blocks.) Clamp the soldered fringe to the soldered rim of the glass using alligator clips or clothespins. Apply more flux and tack solder it in place. Then, go back and add more solder, spreading it smoothly to fill in the gaps in the top. Cut off any excess fringe. Clean and polish.

4

Using round-nosed pliers, twist and curl 14" (36cm) of wire (feel free to use more if you like) into loops to create a handle. Flux both the wire and the rim of the glass where they meet. Solder the wire to the glass.

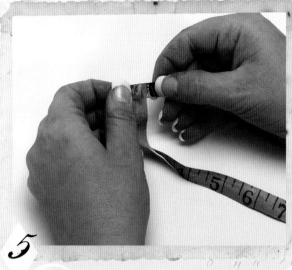

5

Apply copper tape to both ends of ribbon and tape measure scraps. Flux and solder making sure not to touch the ribbon. Solder jump rings, one on each end, to the soldered ends of the ribbon. Clean and polish.

6

Apply copper tape to both ends of the glass dowel. Flux and solder. Solder jump rings to the dowel, one on each end. Clean and polish. Use Diamond Glaze to adhere a word snipped out of an old book for added embellishment. Continue creating fringe elements using found objects. Add beads, charms, keys and so forth to the bottom jump rings of the fringe pieces by wire-wrapping them. Make sure to clean and polish all soldered areas before connecting everything together.

7

Use round-nose pliers to create a carrier for the fringe. This is done by taking a 10" (25cm) piece of wire and alternating bends in it to form a rounded zigzag.

8

After you have created enough "down" zigs to hold an equal amount of fringe pieces, form the zigzaged wire into a ring and cut off any excess wire. Attach the fringe pieces to this wire. Then attach to the jump ring at the bottom of the vase.

Manufacturing Chemists
PHILADELPHIA.

TEST TUBE VASE

Test tubes aren't just for babies anymore! They do a fine job as flower holders, too! Whether you have one in your car, on the refrigerator door or on the flag of your mailbox to surprise Mr. Postman, this is such an easy thing to do and do it you shall! Run out to your local science supply store. Then, come home and make these fun gifts for your 300 closest friends. And remember, if you run out of flowers in your garden, don't be plucking any from your neighbor's garden. . . unless you're sure they're not home!

A Little More: VINTAGE-VESSEL PENDANT

Sometimes, the simplest of elements can be the fanciest of projects. Take for example, a simple vial—the kind used by scientists. Nothing special, nothing fancy. Just a plain glass vial with a black, plastic screw top. Imagine the vial as part of another object. Just consider the possibilities. I did, and that is how I created my glass doll. The vial became her body that one can see within. What secrets are hidden deep inside her? What answers does she hold? She can be opened and filled (or emptied) or just toyed with. Her most brilliant of features, however, is her skirt of found objects that dazzles as she spins. Oh, if only the skirt came in my size!

ingredients

soldering suitcase (see page 22)

vial with screw-on cap, 1" × 3"
(3cm × 8cm)

18"–24" (46cm–61cm) of
16-gauge tinned, copper wire

6" (15cm) of 20-gauge tinned, copper wire

found objects and other items
to make the skirt and her insides

jump rings, 6mm
(quantity depends on fringe)

bisque doll head (with a bit
of a neck still intact)

{1} Clean the vial. Pierce a hole in the top center of the cap. Create a loop at one end of the 20-gauge wire. Feed the other end of the wire up through the cap (from the inside out). Create a loop with the other end of the wire (snip it to an appropriate length). Bend the outside loop down against the lid and cover with a piece of copper tape to hold it in place. (We'll decorate the inside of the doll in a bit.)

{2} Cover the cap with copper tape. Do this by first wrapping the copper tape around the sides of the lid (you may need to make more than one pass). Allow some excess when you wrap it around the cap and fold the excess over onto the top. Cut a circle of copper tape the size of the top of the lid and place it on the center of the lid. Burnish it well. Wrap copper tape around the lower part of the vial about ¼" (6mm) from the bottom and fold over the curved portion, toward the bottom. Burnish as well.

{3} Solder the copper-taped areas. Note: When soldering the plastic cap, do not overheat. This may require stopping and starting so as to allow the cap to cool off.

{4} Grind the neck of the doll head evenly and wrap it with copper tape. Solder this taped area. Place the doll head on top of the cap and tack solder it in place. Then finish the soldering smoothly.

{5} Using the 16-gauge wire, bend it back and forth so as to create a zig-zag with the wire. Wrap it around the base of the vial where the solder is and trim the wire. Tack solder it in place allowing enough of the wire to hang down so the fringe can be attached to it.

{6} With 16-gauge wire, create flowing loops and tack solder it to the neck of the doll, for the chain to hang from. Clean and polish all the soldered areas.

{7} Attach the found objects, chain, fringe and so forth to the zig-zag wire. Fill the inside of the vial with artwork, beads, glitter and more to illustrate the doll's "secrets." Thread a chain through the flowing loop if you would like the doll to be a necklace.

Daily Inspiration Pendant

We all get the blues from time to time. It's a part of the natural cycle of things. But the Land of Sorrow is a place that I refuse to take up shelter in for too terribly long. To bring myself back around, I surround myself with candy necklaces, lighted gooses, and words that make me feel good. And they do. The Daily Inspiration Pendant is the keeper of all that is happy. Within its vial body are strips of linen stamped with words that lighten the load. My personal favorite—TWIRL. Of course, when the words don't work, go shopping! Just CHARGE it! And if nothing else, take a COLD shower and get over it. Since I prefer HOT showers, I let the inspirations and shopping work for me.

little trinkets to make you smile

What inspires me? The side of an old brick building with a painted advertisement barely visible, faded with time. Pieces of an old mirror, the silver crumbling off the back in my hands. A doll whose body is fraying. The ratty fabric on my favorite chair with yellowed stuffing falling out. I am confident that the tear is wider now that my little boy has jumped on it and my cats have scratched at it. This makes me happy. This makes me smile.

Looking around, there is so much to smile about, but you need to notice it first. Concentrate, just for a moment, on how the tree branches sway back and forth in the wind. If you really pay attention, you'll see the green leaves sparkle in the sun—as if they were covered in glitter. Do you see it? Keep watching. Imagine if leaves didn't move—how uninspiring that would be. But as they sway, and sparkle and rustle in the breeze, appreciate it. Smile.

The smallest of things can create the greatest happiness. Imagine a collection of tiny shells, some still dusted in sand, that once upon a time washed ashore and were collected by someone who noticed the little, pinkish treasures nestled against the beach. How happy would you be if there was a collection of these sandy seashells spilling around inside an antique bottle reincarnated into a pendant to wear and fondle all day long.

I know you're looking out your window right now. Paying attention to the leaves. Yes. Yes—you are smiling! I just know it. But don't stop there. Turn the page and you will see little trinkets designed to make you happy. It may be the tiny silver chair that you can cover with your own tattered fabric. Or possibly, the tiny book to fill with lists of things that make you smile because you've begun noticing them. Without a doubt, it may be the tiny bottle relic that holds a collection of seashells floured in sand. You'll shake it in your hand and imagine yourself there, at the very beach where they came from—the sun beating down and casting a shadow of you on the sand, the wind gently blowing your hair across your face. You'll feel as if you are there. And you'll smile.

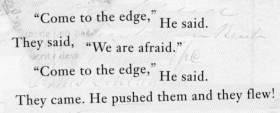

"Come to the edge," He said.
They said, "We are afraid."
"Come to the edge," He said.
They came. He pushed them and they flew!

Guillaume Apollinaire

Pendant

So. You're currently out of solder, but still need a new, dangly bit of jewelry? It's time for a solder-free solution! Not only is this a great project to make that doesn't need electricity (well, not a lot of electricity—you still need light to see), this is a great project when you want to work with transparencies, unusual glass or etching. Since the Edgeless Pendant is created in layers, there are many opportunities to try different techniques. In fact, if you liked musical chairs as a child, you could use this technique to play musical pendants. Mix and match dozens of pieces of glass with unique artwork to finally come up with three pieces of glass and artwork, images, ephemera, fabric, and more, sandwiched inside. Have fun mixing. Have fun matching. Have fun walking on the edge!

Want more?

Make all of the images that are part of this pendant transparent. Then the pendant will be entirely see-through. Or, instead of paper, use a snippet of lace trim or a pressed flower. Perhaps the middle piece is made of mirror (for those moments when you need to touch up your lipstick).

ingredients

collage cargo (see page 19)

1/16" (2mm) window glass and/or decorative clear glass

transparency (artwork or text)

20-gauge sterling silver wire

wire cutters

round-nose pliers

leather cord, 30" (76cm)

1

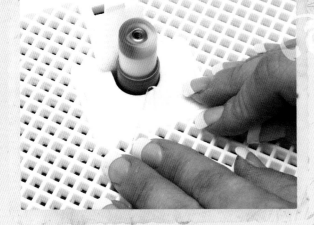

Cut the glass into three identical sizes approximately 1³/₈" × 1⁷/₈" (3cm × 5cm). For this project I used one piece of regular window glass and two pieces of vintage-like, window glass with bubbles and imperfections. This type of glass can be found at a stained-glass store, but also consider the recycling bins of a neighbor's house that is being renovated. Grind the edges of the glass smooth, and to round the corners, carefully push the sharp corner of the first piece of glass into the bit. Move it back and forth to create a rounded corner. Grind along the rounded edges so that they are smooth as well. Make sure to wear safety glass or, for a real fashion statement, full head gear.

2

Using the glass as a guide, cut the transparency (purchased or made by you) to the shape of the glass.

3

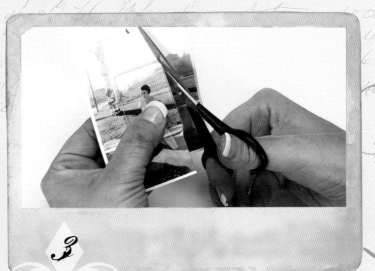

Again, using the glass as a guide, cut a vintage photo to the size of the glass. Repeat for one or two various papers, but remember, you do not want any 3-dimensional imagery for this project. If you would like to use a collage as your artwork, have a laser-color copy made or scan it on your computer and print it out.

4

Use adhesive to glue two images together to create back-to-back artwork.

5

Double-check all your trim sizes with the glass, to see if you need to clean up the edges with scissors.

You're now ready to layer the pieces in this order: glass, transparency, glass, back-to-back image, glass. Use a drop of Diamond Glaze on each of the four corners to secure the images to the glass. Let dry. All three pieces of glass and all images should be glued to each other in one stack, like a triple-decker sandwich.

6

7

Cut a 10" (25cm) length of wire. Create a loop with a round-nose pliers approximately 1½" (4cm) from the end. Hold the wire so that the loop is centered at the top of the glass and bend the long length of wire around the glass toward the back (on the side). Bring it back to the front at the center-bottom, then to the back again at the opposite side in the center. Eventually, bring it to the top where the loop is. The wire should be wrapped tightly as if it were the only thing holding the glass and artwork together.

8

Twist both ends of the excess wire around the loop.

9

Cut off any remaining excess. Thread the cord through the loop to create a pendant.

CREATE

If I can solder plastic ballerinas to a tiara, I can solder just about anything—and do. That is why it is such a challenge to find ways to connect objects without the ease of soldering. Normally, I would copper tape these two pieces of beveled glass and solder them to create a pendant. Instead, I wrapped them with page numbers from the table of contents of an old book and sealed them with Diamond Glaze. Then, I bent wire into a zig-zag all around the pendant. Now, let me just say that this sounds easier than it is. I've since discovered that I'm not a zig-zag bender type of girl. But, I did take a walk on the wild side and this is one pretty pendant (soldered or not)!

I take the view, and always have,
that if you cannot say what you're going to say
in twenty minutes you ought to go away
and write a book about it.

Lord Brabazon

UNTOLD-STORYBOOK
Pendant

"SOMETIMES THERE WAS A STORM IN HER BRAIN"—my mantra! Of course, as soon as the storm comes in, it goes back out. Therefore, no matter where I went (out for a romantic dinner, to the park, shopping and out for Strawberry Drops with girlfriends . . .) I would always bring my custom-made, oblong journal and a fine-point permanent marker, ready to jot this or that down at a moment's notice. But, after downsizing my purses (what a chore that was!), my trusty sidekick (the "book-book") no longer met all of my needs. Enter the StoryBook Pendant! A perfect way to capture fleeting thoughts and look stunning, too. Showcasing your cover artwork as it dangles around your neck, you'll find yourself often taking it in your hand, opening it and capturing some great idea (or at least the two items you would otherwise forget at the grocery store). Create one, or better yet, create a dozen—just for your own storms!

ingredients

collage cargo (see page 19)

soldering suitcase (see page 22)

gesso

miniature book (such as a Christmas tree ornament, no more than 3" high and ½" thick [8cm × 1cm])

1/16" (2mm) window glass

jump ring (8mm to 9mm)

necklace chain (or ribbon), 30" (76cm) or longer

Want more?

To attach a pencil to the book, cut a standard pencil down to 3" (8cm) (or use golf-scoring pencils). Wrap the top ½" (13mm) of the pencil in copper tape and solder it. Attach a jump ring to the top. Hook one end of an open link chain to the pencil's jump ring and the other end to the book's jump ring. Voila!

1

Begin with a cheap, silly little ornament book from the dollar store. Alter the existing miniature book by applying gesso to the interior pages, painting, stamping, gluing vintage papers and photographs, sanding and embellishing to your heart's content. Make sure to adorn the front and back covers in a breathtaking fashion as they will be visible while dangling around your neck. Don't forget that there will be a border of soldered, copper tape around the covers, so make sure any important text or artwork is about 1/8" (3mm) away from the border. When finished, let dry completely.

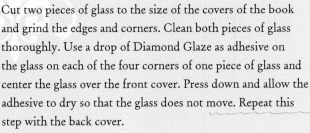

2

Cut two pieces of glass to the size of the covers of the book and grind the edges and corners. Clean both pieces of glass thoroughly. Use a drop of Diamond Glaze as adhesive on the glass on each of the four corners of one piece of glass and center the glass over the front cover. Press down and allow the adhesive to dry so that the glass does not move. Repeat this step with the back cover.

Wrap the covers with copper tape. The tape should go over the edges of the glass book cover and be folded down on the inside covers. Extra copper tape may be needed on the spine. However, do not completely cover the spine with copper tape as, when soldered, it will not open. Burnish the copper tape flat. Solder all the copper tape beginning with the inside covers first, being careful not to get flux on the book.

3

Solder a jump ring to the top of the spine. Clean and polish.

Cut a piece of text from an old book (or use any vintage paper) that is 1/8" to 1/16" (3mm to 2mm) smaller on all sides than the spine. Apply caulk to the backside of that text and press along the spine to cover up the unsoldered area. Apply caulk over the top of the text and let dry. Caulk is used as the sealant here since it is flexible and will allow the book to open and close. String the chain through the jump ring and wear it as a necklace.

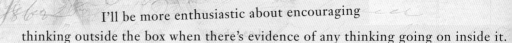

I'll be more enthusiastic about encouraging
thinking outside the box when there's evidence of any thinking going on inside it.

Terry Pratchett

Pendant

IT'S JUST THE ARTFUL THING TO DO—think outside the box.
To do the unexpected. To create the unusual. Just don't forget, once in awhile,
it's OK to think *inside* the box, too. Don't fret—this won't limit you—
there are four "insides" to play with. Let your imagination run wild. Four
people to immortalize. Four stories to tell. Four flowers to preserve.
Four games to play. Think outside the box and inside the box at the
same time, but don't think too hard—ouch!

ingredients

collage cargo (see page 19)

soldering suitcase (see page 22)

small jewelry box lids, 2

1/16" (2mm) window glass

jump rings (8mm to 9mm), 2

necklace chain (or ribbon), 30"
(76cm) or longer

*Create movement inside the box by placing loose beads in one
section. Write words on the beads and make a game
of it by trying to shake them into a sentence.*

1

Use scissors to cut the long sides off each lid. Do this by measuring the height of the lid and drawing a line at that same distance from the side, along the interior top of the box. This will form a long wedge. Do this for each of the two boxes, which will give you four triangular sides.

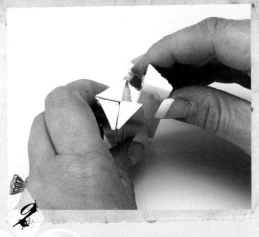

2

Glue the wedges together using clear caulk, so that they form a rectangular shape with openings on all four sides. You'll be tempted to begin right away—but let the caulk set.

3

Use collage supplies to create artwork in the four alcoves of the box. Three-dimensional pieces can be added, provided that they do not stick out so far as to potentially interfere with the glass cover.

4

Cut one piece of glass to fit slightly larger than each of the four sides (measure and cut each one separately—they may not all be exactly the same), grind any rough corners and clean. Carefully apply adhesive along the box edges, and press the glass into place. Let sit to dry, and then move on to glue the next side until all four sides are covered in glass.

5

Cut four strips of copper tape, (⅜" [10mm] or wider if necessary) that are the same height as the box. Center the tape along each of the four corners, making sure that the edges of the glass are covered. Burnish smooth.

Cut a piece of copper sheet approximately ¼" (6mm) larger on all sides than the top and bottom of the box. This is best done by placing the top (or bottom) of the box on the copper sheet and using an awl to scribe into the copper. (The box may not be perfectly square so just cutting a perfect square may not work perfectly.) Place the cut copper sheet on the top and fold the sides over at 90-degree angles. Make sure to fold the corners in, as if wrapping a gift. Burnish smooth. Solder the sides, top and bottom. Solder a jump ring to the top center of the box. Use a third hand jewelry tool to hold the jump ring while you tack solder it in place.

6

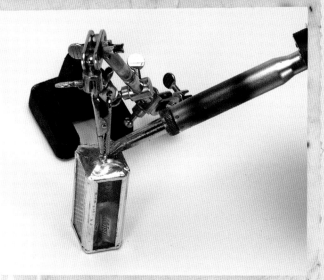

7

Prop the box upside down, between two metal blocks and solder a jump ring to the bottom center of the box. Clean and polish. If you like, you can use wire to attach a bead dangle or crystal from the jump ring at the bottom of the box. String the chain through the top jump ring and wear it as a necklace.

SHE'S ON A PEDESTAL, YET AGAIN

Only trophy wives were ever on pedestals—until now! This little dear who inhabits a 4-way box shrine sits atop a pedestal—the base of a very sassy martini glass. What's sad for the martini is glad for the girl! Each section is like a store window offering a peek at goodies inside. An antique doll head from Germany tops a stack of old thread, a porcelain letter A, tidbits here and there. All are bound together with solder and topped with a beveled diamond previewing the story inside. A little silk ribbon finishes her off (just like she wished she'd finished off the martini!).

Manufacturing Chemists
PHILADELPHIA.

FAMILY FOUR-WAY

These days, families seem to get lost, in general. You know it's gone way off the deep end when your daughter instant messages you to ask if she can go out over the weekend, and your son calls you on your cell phone (from upstairs) to ask if dinner is ready. Bring back the family. Record your favorite parts about being a family in the four sides of this pendant. Make up a word that hasn't been invented yet! "Remembry"—a cross between remember and memory. Keep a tally it your own "Family Dictionary." Then, after making milkshakes for dinner, make this treasure to wear next to your heart and treasure the simple things. Say "I love you." Always say "I love you." Every day. At least once.

He who loses money loses much. He who loses a friend loses more.

But he who loses faith loses all.

Henry H. Haskins

Pendant

I love the
truth
and
peace

FAITH. I'VE ALWAYS HAD IT—even though some days I think I've lost it. I believe everyone has faith; the confident belief in the truth, value, or trustworthiness of a person, idea or thing. Faith: a belief that does not rest on logical proof or material evidence. To illustrate my faith, I felt compelled to create a cross that was both beautiful and meaningful. Preserved under glass is imagery that moves me. When I wear it, I am not alone. When I don't, it hangs in a special place where I can reflect upon it, should I ever lose faith.

ingredients

collage cargo (see page 19)

soldering suitcase (see page 22)

1/16" (2mm) window glass

jump ring (7mm)

necklace chain (or ribbon), 30" (76cm) or longer

Want more?

Contemplate putting prayers within the sections of the cross, meaningful passages that you can reflect upon daily.

1

Cut six ¾" (2cm) strips of glass that are 1¼" (3cm) long and two ¾" (2cm) strips that are 2¼" (6cm) long. Cut two ½" (13mm) squares. Grind all the corners lightly. To achieve more curvature in the strips (like I have here), grind the shapes with an electric grinder so that the strip narrows to ½" (13mm) wide. Keep in mind that the pieces need to sandwich together and be exactly the same shape.

Use the cut-glass shapes as a template to cut out your artwork (which should be two-sided). Clean the glass and sandwich the artwork between it.

2

Wrap each glass piece with copper tape, making sure that the seam is at the short side (which will connect with the center square). Solder each piece individually. Lay the cross out, beginning with the center square (just like *Hollywood Squares*), with the front sides facing up. Tack solder all the pieces together. Flip the cross over and tack solder the back pieces together. Then flip it back so the front is facing up, and apply a nice, smooth, soldered finish where all the sides meet. Flip it to the back and smooth the joints with solder. Prop the cross so it is standing straight up and down and attach a jump ring to the top center of the cross. Clean and polish. Thread the finished cross onto the necklace chain.

TIMELESS SIGNIFICANCE

When my husband's grandmother died, the only thing he wanted from the estate was the cross which hung in her home—Easter palms still attached. Crosses aren't just thrown away or sold at garage sales. They are handed down from generation to generation. The larger of these two crosses is mine. Beveled-glass shapes were filled with beautiful words and illustrations from antique Bibles, scavenged from here and France. It rests in our home atop a pair of Bibles that survived the Great Chicago Fire and were given to me by my Grandmother. I know she would approve.

The smaller piece (fitted with my favorite vintage ribbon), is a remembrance of unanswerable things that happened once upon a time, and a symbol of what you can count on in the future.

As I was sitting in my chair,

I knew the bottom wasn't there,

Nor legs nor back, but I just sat, Ignoring little things like that.

Hughes Mearns

de Francé

"OUI! TRÉS BONNE CHAISE!" It had been two years since she visited Paris, but she remembered it like it was yesterday. Lucky enough to have a best friend who would take her along on such a jaunt, the two girls packed everything but the kitchen sink for ten days of merveilleux. They gallivanted throughout the "City of Lights," making sure to visit Chanel (what cute "doorboys"), order eclairs, and spend an entire day walking from Notre Dame to the Eiffel Tower (it seemed so close when they started). An afternoon lounging by the pond at le Jardin du Luxembourg and making up stories about the Parisians passing by was topped only by lunch at a corner café. As they sat outside in pretty, little French chairs, taking a bite of croque monsieur (France's answer to a ham and cheese sandwich) and drinking $5 diet sodas, they giggled to each other, "This is the life!"

ingredients

collage cargo (see page 19)

soldering suitcase (see page 22)

1/16" (2mm) window glass

16-gauge wire (tinned copper or sterling silver)

wire cutters

round-nose pliers

needle-nose pliers

jump ring (7mm)

fabric or ribbon

Want more?

Create an entire collection of tables and chairs. Make large chairs and small chairs. Let the upholstery be snippets of vintage clothing, found ribbons or favorite lace trims. This is a great project for fabric as the texture on the chair is beautiful.

1

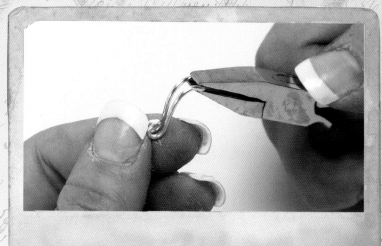

2

Cut two pieces of glass into rectangles approximately
1" × ½" (3cm × 1cm). With a permanent marker, draw
identical ovals that expand to each edge. Grind these
down into matching oval shapes using an electric
grinder. (See Glass-Cutting Greatness, pages 20–21.)
Cut 2 pieces of glass approximately ⅞" × 1⅛" (22mm
x 3cm). With a permanent marker, draw two identical
trapezoids to fit within the glass. Grind these down
into matching shapes with rounded corners. Using the
glass as a template, cut artwork to fit. Keep in mind that
both sides of the glass are visible, so make your artwork
two-sided.

Clean the glass and apply copper tape to both sections of the chair. The seam should be at the point
where the chair back meets the seat. Fold the tape down
carefully so both the front and the back are covered
equally. Burnish smooth. Solder both pieces individually. Clean and polish.

Cut wire into two 2½" (6cm) pieces. Using round-
nose pliers, bend the wire in half. Use wire cutters to
square off the raw ends of the wire. Use round-nose
pliers to twirl the raw ends to make matching loops
(this should mimic claw-feet on furniture).

Use needle-nose pliers to bend the wire at the middle point.
This should make a soft right angle (as shown) and give the leg
of the chair some curvature. Do this for both 2½" (6cm) pieces
of wire to form the front legs.

3

Cut two 1½" (4cm) long pieces of wire. Use round-nose
pliers to twirl a little loop on one end of each piece of wire.
Twirl a slightly larger loop into the other end of the wire.
Use needle-nose pliers to bend the larger loop to the side
at a 90-degree angle (as shown). These form the back legs.

4

Lay the seat of the chair upside down. Use pliers to hold the front legs in place. Apply solder to the legs and the chair where they will connect. Solder the connection carefully. Note: You can adjust the height of the legs by rolling the feet higher or lower with round-nose pliers when the chair is completed. When doing this, use the flat pliers to hold the wire leg to the chair at the soldered point, since it is fragile.

5

Solder the back legs to the chair in the same fashion, making sure that the loops of the feet curve outward. Lay the seat of the chair on the table so that the front legs and front of the chair are on the table, and the back legs are in the air. Use pliers to hold the back of the chair against the center back of the seat. Apply flux and tack solder in place. Turn the chair upside down and tack solder the inside bend where the chair back meets the seat. Then, turn it back over and finish soldering the back. Note: Do not leave the iron on the chair too long or it may re-melt some of the solder and individual pieces of the chair may fall off. Stand the chair upright and solder a jump ring to the center top of the oval. Clean and polish.

Manufacturing Chemists
PHILADELPHIA.

LA MAISON

This house is a castle in every sense of the word! It is also a labor of love (I seem to have a lot of those lately). I got most excited about it when I realized it was a cross between art and decorating . . .in the truest sense of the word. Scouring old catalogs and magazines for just the right "lamp" and "chair" and "fireplace!" My goodness! The fireplace! One can't help but notice the logs are ready for a romantic evening at home. Different from my home? Color scheme . . .no. Lack of laundry on the floor . . . yes. Building this house requires patience and tenacity. To build it correctly, accurate measurements are a must.

Monsieur

199 Boulevard Volt

Paris

DUVAL.
TOME SECOND.

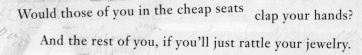

Would those of you in the cheap seats   clap your hands?

And the rest of you, if you'll just rattle your jewelry.

John Lennon

Bracelet

MY MOTHER GAVE ME MY VERY OWN STERLING SILVER charm bracelet, adorned with a few charms that would convey meaning—among them, a cat. It was so grown-up and expensive-feeling. Throughout the years, certain occasions would add certain charms to the bracelet such as the state of New York (after a summer visit), a "Happy Birthday" message, even a clarinet. (I played it once upon a time.) This was the beginning of my love for small, meaningful, shiny objects.

It is time for me to pass the tradition on to my daughter and give her a charm bracelet of her very own. However, now I am lucky enough to embellish it with charms that hold photographs of her friends and family, snippets of her baby blanket, and a special note from me to her. Someday, I know it might be tucked away in a box in the back of a drawer, but there will come a time when she will find it again—and remember.

Want more?

Use lobster clasps to attach charms to your bracelet, so you can hook them on securely and take them off at will. This way, you can make dozens (or hundreds) of charms and wear only a few, carefully selected charms each day, to suit your mood.

ingredients

soldering suitcase (see page 22)

dimensional elements for charms

jump rings, 6mm, (quantity varies with chosen number of charms)

sterling, chunk-chain bracelet

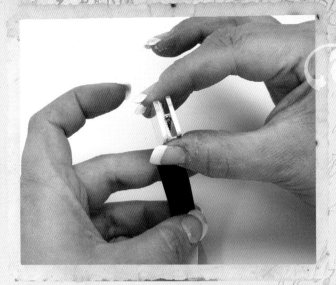

1

To make a three-dimensional item like a short string of rhinestones into a charm, begin by cutting two 1" (3cm) square pieces of glass. Grind the edges and corners. Using the glass as a template, cut a piece of vintage paper and a piece of velvet ribbon to the size of the glass. Glue the paper to the back of the velvet ribbon. Using adhesive caulk, adhere the rhinestones to the center of the ribbon. Clean the glass. With the object between the glass, balance the two pieces between your fingers so the glass is evenly spaced on all four sides. Starting at the seam at the top of the charm, lay the glass on the sticky side of copper tape so that it is centered. Roll the charm in the copper tape taking care to keep the glass pieces spaced equally apart. Fold the edges over making sure that the corners are folded in at 90-degree angles (hospital corners). Burnish gently until smooth. Be careful not to press any one side too hard, as the glass may cave in. Prop the charm between locking pliers to keep it steady and solder the taped areas. Use pliers to solder a jump ring to the top. Clean and polish.

2

For a button, or any other item that you want to "float" in the center of the charm, secure it to a piece of glass with just a tiny dab of clear caulk or Diamond Glaze. Then, repeat from step 1.

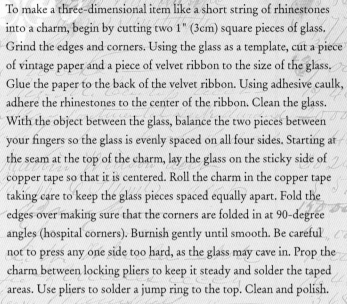

3

For many found objects (that aren't plastic) such as typewriter keys or game pieces, you don't even need glass just tape the object itself, then solder. If you decide to work with plastic, don't heat it for too long at any given time. Let it cool often by placing it against the wet sponge, and take your time.

4

For oval or round charms, cut two square (or rectangular) pieces of glass so that all sides are the same size. Grind the corners down so that it forms an oval or circle. Make sure that both pieces of glass are equally shaped.

(OPTIONAL TECHNIQUE): Use a hand circle cutter to create circles of equal size. The circle cutter is limited to circles no smaller than the size of a nickel. To create smaller circles, see Step 4 (above).

A Little More:
HISTORY JUST HANGING AROUND

If we could have a bowl of found objects, it would have to be a crystal one where the light can shine through. It would also have to be a chipped one, as only something unwanted by others could coddle small objects so tenderly. Piled in the bowl would be a single granny earring—the clip-on type—where its mate long ago lost. Maybe a small metal pill box, rusty with age. A domino found in the seat cushions of the sofa, long after the game it belonged to was sold for 5 cents at that garage sale you had last summer. Here, in the pretty bowl, one-of-a-kind, two-of-a-kind, and handfuls of tiny treasures await their next adventure in life. It is with the objects in my bowl (not crystal—but definitely tarnished and bent silver) that I discovered the little treasures that found new life around my neck.

No. 15—SUBTRACT

5

ingredients

soldering suitcase (see page 22)

sterling or faux chain

jump rings (6mm or 7mm)
sterling, silver-plated, or nickel wire

{1} For the domino, wrap it in copper tape and solder it entirely. Attach jump rings to both of the short ends. Remember, dominos need not stay rectangular . . .they can be cut in half to make individual squares.

{2} For the letter cube, use a drill press or a hand drill to make a small hole through the center. Feed a length of wire through the hole and create loops on both ends by first creating a loop with your round-nose pliers, then winding the excess wire around it.

{3} For the marble, cut standard ⅜" (10mm) copper tape into narrower strips (⅛" [3mm] or less) with your scissors. Wrap the tape around the marble, making sure to overlap at the ends. You will wrap two pieces of tape all the way around the marble to section it off in quarters (like quartering an orange). Burnish and solder as usual. Solder jump rings to both ends (where all four pieces of tape meet.)

{4} The vintage metal numbers were found with holes already in them . . .but nearly anything can have a hole drilled through it with the use of the correct tool. When drilling glass and stone, make sure to use a diamond bit with water (and be patient). Of course, if drilling isn't your thing, find a friend, a friend of a friend, or a local store that can assist you.

{5} With the addition of copper tape to nearly any object, the ends can be soldered and jump rings attached so even the most elusive of found objects can find its way onto your special necklace. Attach the soldered jump rings on the charms to the links of the necklace.

Storybook Bracelet

As if I didn't jingle enough, I just had to create a bracelet that would jingle more! And jingle it does! Twenty tiny charms made from microscope slide glass are attached to a chunky link bracelet. Microscope slides are thinner than the window glass I typically use, so the bracelet is a little lighter and it clangs a little differently. Even better, the artwork inside each charm is actually a French version of a Dick-and-Jane book, which I cut up to use its illustrations as the pictures. For a girl who has cut up many a Dick-and-Jane book (much to my mother's horror, I'm sure), I finally took the leap and cut up the special French version. But Mom . . . I haven't cut up my "Stories About Sally" Dick-and-Jane book that you gave me. . . yet!

Aerodynamically the bumblebee shouldn't be able to fly,
but the bumblebee doesn't know it,
so it goes on flying anyway.

Mary Kay Ash

FLY-AWAY
Pin

IT'S A BUG'S LIFE. That lucky, little dragonfly. Spending days and nights outdoors. Zipping through flower gardens, perching on some zinnia or delphinium, basking in the sun. That dragonfly would be just as lucky spending an afternoon clinging to your sweater, traveling with you to lunch with the girls, enjoying a Strawberry Drop at the infamous Paragon. Oh, yes, a dragonfly of your very own. And here's how to create one!

ingredients

soldering suitcase (see page 22)

scrap of vintage paper or decorative tissue paper

chunks of broken safety glass (glass store or glass repair shop—they usually have leftover scraps that get thrown away)

Diamond Glaze and brush

16-gauge wire (tinned copper or sterling silver)

20-gauge wire
(tinned copper or sterling silver

wire cutters

round-nose pliers

epoxy

1" (3cm) silver-toned pin back

Want more?

If you enjoy this project, try creating an entire family of bug pins—bees, flies, spiders and so on.

From your stash of broken safety glass, find two pieces that mimic the shape of a dragonfly's body and tail and won't require too much grinding to shape them. Gently grind the edges smooth and into shapes for the body and the tail. Use a grinding machine for best results. Make sure to wear safety glasses.

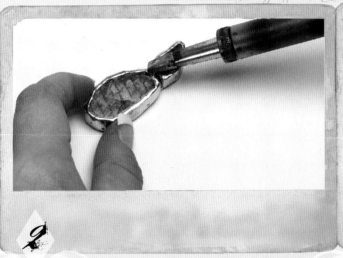

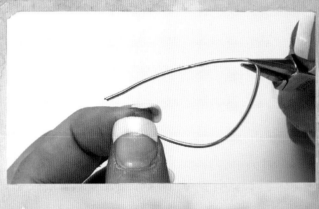

2

Trim vintage paper or tissue paper to the shapes of the body. Brush Diamond Glaze on one side of the glass. Press the decorative paper onto the glass with the decorative side against the glass. Let dry and trim. Apply three or four more coats of Diamond Glaze, allowing it to dry between coats. Apply copper tape around the sides of the glass (½" [13mm] copper tape may be best for thicker safety glass). Fold the edges down and burnish. Make sure the seam is located where the body meets the tail as it will not be visible there. Solder both the tail and the body separately. Then, lay the two pieces next to each other to form the dragonfly shape and tack solder into place. Fill in any gaps with additional solder. Clean and polish.

3

Cut four 5" (13cm) pieces of 16-gauge wire. Using your hands and round-nose pliers, shape the wire into two sets of wings (the top wings being larger than the bottom wings).

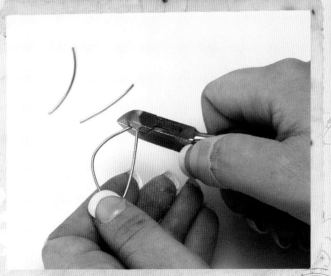

4

Use wire cutters to cut the ends of the wings flush.

5

Place each set of wings on an anvil (metal block) and hammer the round wire flat.

6

Use a helping hand to hold one of the wings in place. Apply flux to both the ends of the wire and the body of the dragonfly, where the wings will be attached. Then, apply drops of solder to the wire where it meets the body in order to attach it. Do this for all four wings.

7

Flux one end of a 6" (15cm) length of 20-gauge wire and solder it to the body where a wing meets it.

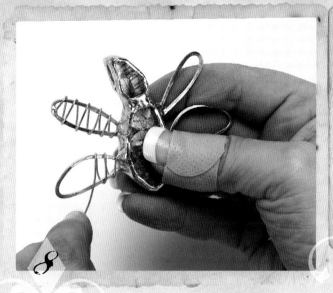

8

Then wrap the 20-gauge wire around the wing as tightly or loosely as you desire. This not only finishes off the wings, but creates a "cage" where in you can tuck a little note, photograph, or scrap of fabric.

9

Cut off the excess wire when you get to the end of the wing and flux the end as well as the portion of the wing it will be attached to. Solder the wire to the end of the wing. Do this for all four wings. To make the cute little antanna, cut one piece of 16-gauge wire about 3" (7cm) in length and bend it into a U shape that is flat on the bottom. Flux the center as well as the front of the dragonfly's body and solder the U wire to the body. Fan the antenna outward and cut to the desired length. Use round-nose pliers to coil the ends and create little loops. Clean and polish. Use epoxy to attach the pin finding to the back of the dragonfly's body (the back is the part with the artwork on it). You'll be tempted to let the dragonfly perch on your shoulder right away, but be sure to let him dry first!

FLUTTER PENDANTS

Who likes bugs? Not many. Let's just say these aren't bugs. They're birds that were misrouted! Yeah, that's it! And these little girlies like to flutter about, showing off their artful wings. It is the wings that make them so attractive—the flowing shape, the brilliant colors, the speed at which they move! To capture the color, antique dragonfly prints were scanned in and printed on tissue paper. Wire was bent to the outline shape of the printed wings and after the wire was attached to the body of the Dragonfly with solder, the wings were cut out and glued to the edges of the wire with Diamond Glaze. Here's a tip: if you cut out the wings a little larger and glue them down, after the adhesive is dry you can wet the excess tissue paper and easily tear it off. Even if we do concede that dragonflies are really bugs, not birds, they, actually, are pretty pretty.

AN ORNAMENT

AN INSECT

Many have fallen with the bottle in their hand.

Native American Proverb

BEAUTILICIOUS-SODA-BOTTLE
Bracelet

So YOU'RE STRUGGLING with recycling. Your 16-year-old son isn't taking care of the bottles and cans like he's supposed to? Don't just cut off his allowance! Instead make a special bracelet to console yourself for getting stuck with his chores. Well, enough about my life! But if you feel my pain, enjoy this special treat! Save wine bottles, ask for empty liquor bottles from your favorite restaurant, shop antique stores for vintage bottles. You'll never pass by a pretty bottle again.

ingredients

collage cargo (see page 19)

soldering suitcase (see page 22)

soda bottle (or other glass bottle)

1" (3cm) silk ribbon
20" (51cm) toggle clasp

jump rings (7mm or 8mm), 2

Want more?

Make several curved charms and string them together on one bracelet or necklace, using ribbon or jump rings.

1

From a soda, wine or other glass bottle (here, we used a Jones Soda bottle), score the bottom of the bottle with a hand glass cutter and tap it to knock out the bottom. Use a glass ring saw to cut a line perpendicular to the bottom of the bottle ⅝" to ¾" (16mm to 19mm) deep, then rock the bottle left or right to cut sideways for approximately 2" (5cm). Then pull back out. This will leave you with a piece of curved glass that is about ¾" × 2" (2cm × 5cm).

2

Carefully snap the piece from the bottle after it is cut. Then cut another piece from the bottle in the same manner, but just a bit shorter (1⅞" [5cm]).

3

What, no ring? If you don't have a ring saw, some stained-glass stores will allow you to use theirs for a fee or they will cut the bottle for you. Another option is to score the bottle by hand and cut a 4" (10cm) strip. Then, score and cut that strip in half.

4

Grind both pieces with a grinder until smooth and even in width with one another. One piece should be slightly shorter than the other, so that when they nest inside each other, the edges are evenly matched. Trim a photo, or other piece of artwork to fit behind the glass, then back it with a piece of vintage or decorative paper. Clean the glass and place the completed artwork between the two pieces of glass.

Apply copper tape around the edges. It's best to cut four pieces of copper tape slightly longer than the edges that they will go on. First, tape the straight (shortest) sides making sure to fold the corners down at 90-degree angles. Then, tape the long, curved sides. This is best done by placing the tape on the outside of the curve first, then folding it onto the edge and lastly over to the back (inside curve). Fold these corners at 90-degree angles also. Burnish smooth.

5

Solder the copper taped areas. Solder the jump rings to the short sides of the charm. Clean and polish.

6

Cut the silk ribbon in half. Put one end of the ribbon through one of the jump rings and knot it. Do the same with the end of the other half of the silk ribbon. It is optional if you want to cut the excess off (or tuck it in). Place the bracelet (as it is) on your wrist and judge where you would like the findings to be so that the bracelet will fit not too loosely or too tightly. Thread the other end of the ribbon through one part of the toggle clasp and tie a knot in it. Do the same with the other side of the bracelet and its ribbon. Make sure the bracelet fits just right before cutting off any excess.

BOTTLE BANGLE

The gracious curves of a bottle need not be limited to forming charms. This bracelet was made from an entire portion of a pretty decorative bottle. The bottle was scored and cut into two portions to make the break easier.

MORE CURVES

Bottles are plentiful, and I just couldn't resist cutting more up. Yet another Jones Soda bottle is turned into a sassy bracelet by cutting the curved glass into small squares. Bits from antique books were glazed to the back of each single piece of glass. After taping and soldering each individual square, two jump rings were then soldered to each of the two non-curved sides of the glass. Then, they were hooked together using one additional jump ring. Of course, the outer charms only had a single jump ring soldered to the center to hold the clasp. This same technique can be done with non-curved glass.

If we keep treating our most important values as meaningless relics that's exactly what they'll become.

Michael Josephson

LIFE'S-A-BEACH
Pendant

Summers spent at Jamesport. A little cottage, just a stone's throw from the Long Island shore. A sleeping porch big enough for a dozen cousins. A grassy backyard surrounded by a white picket fence, the clothesline strewn with dripping swimsuits. Rock painting. Seashell collecting. Jellyfish hunting. The waves pounding the shore, chasing the sand away, and sinking back into the ocean again . . . .These are the days that make a childhood memorable. My childhood.

I found myself yearning to capture those moments. Those memories. In the spirit of ancient reliquaries found in Italy, I created my own container of relics in the round that holds mementos that mean the most. You, too, can create a reliquary in the round to hold your most precious memories.

ingredients

soldering suitcase (see page 22)

glass vial or bottle approximately
1½" in diameter (4cm)

1/16" window glass (enough to cut 2 circles)

16-gauge wire (tinned copper or sterling silver)

wire cutters

round-nose pliers

epoxy

miniature found objects
(here, sand and shells)

necklace chain

Want more?

This is the perfect vessel to hold your child's first lost tooth, a bit of trim from your wedding gown, a fortune from the fortune cookie you ate on your first date with your husband, a tiny rhinestone pin you wore to the prom. Even silly things say a lot: a pink Barbie shoe, a toy diamond ring, glitter . . .

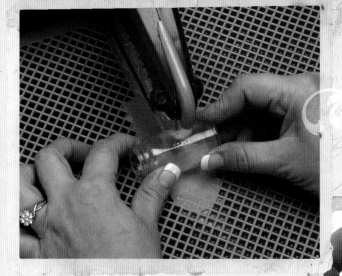

1

Using a ring saw, cut a 1" (3cm) ring from the bottle or vial. Grind the edges smooth and flat.

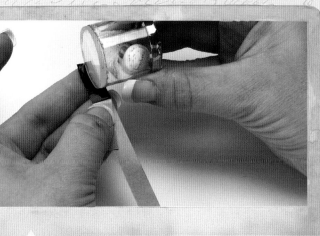

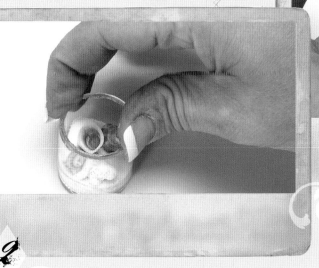

3

Apply copper tape to the edges of the ring. It is important that the copper tape cover the flat glass sides completely, especially the rough edges and where it connects with the ring as this further prevents any of the particles of sand (or other ingredients) from escaping. Also, make sure the seams for both sides end up in the same lateral location (they will be covered up with wire). Burnish smooth.

2

Cut a piece of window glass into a circle with a circle cutter the same diameter as the bottle and grind the edges smooth. Clean all pieces of glass. Using a toothpick, apply epoxy around the rough edge of the ring. Carefully place one round piece of glass on the ring so that it is connected with the adhesive. Let dry completely. Fill the vessel with your most precious miniatures. Here, we've placed tiny shells scavenged from an old necklace and white sand inside to create a "beachy" memory. Add tiny words to some of your objects if you like. It is important not to overfill it, so as to hamper the motion of the goodies inside .

Flux and solder the copper-taped areas. Clean and polish. Cut a 6" (15cm) length of wire. Use round-nose pliers to hold the wire in the center while bending it to create a loop.

4

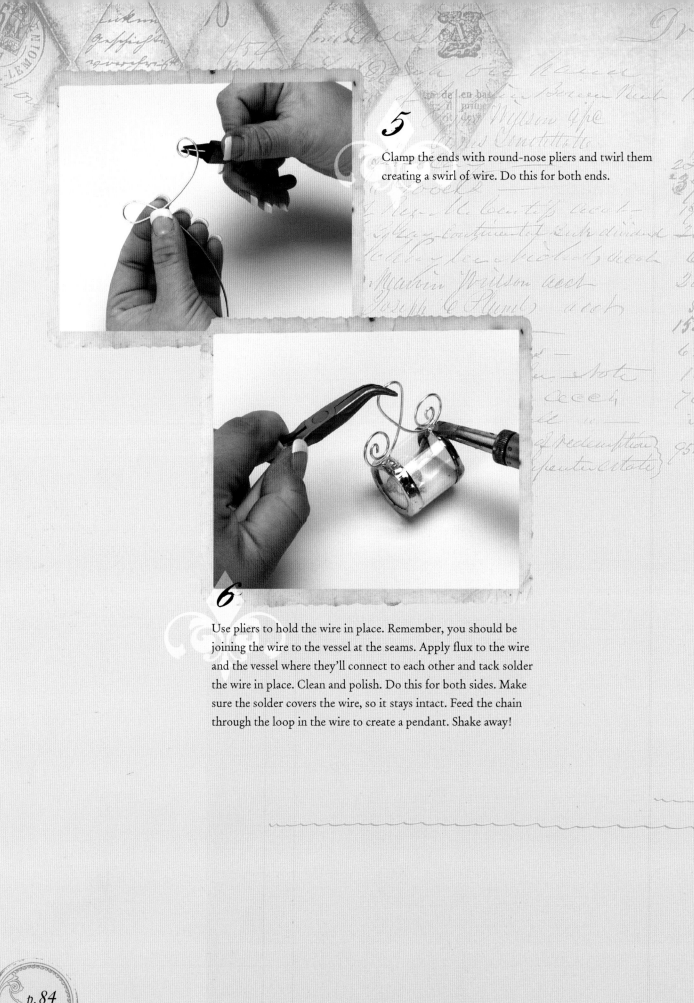

5

Clamp the ends with round-nose pliers and twirl them creating a swirl of wire. Do this for both ends.

6

Use pliers to hold the wire in place. Remember, you should be joining the wire to the vessel at the seams. Apply flux to the wire and the vessel where they'll connect to each other and tack solder the wire in place. Clean and polish. Do this for both sides. Make sure the solder covers the wire, so it stays intact. Feed the chain through the loop in the wire to create a pendant. Shake away!

THE MORE, THE MERRIER

Obsession is good. And lately, the objects of my obsession are things in miniature. Thus, my current obsession with reliquaries and the treasures they hold. As I cut up each bottle on Big Red (my pet name for my glass saw), some of the smaller bottles weren't getting much action (not to mention the thin necks of the larger bottles). Then, like a lightening bolt, it hit me. What's good for the goose is good for the gander. Well, not that exact thought. But why not make the relics smaller—bracelet sized—so one could enjoy several at a time!

OVAL RELIQUARY

Unbelievable but true, this pendant was made from a glass canister found at a discount import store. Its shape is common, but unusual at the same time. Within it are pearls of different sizes rescued from broken necklaces. Each one has a different word adhered to it that is part of a phrase, "I wish to remind you that one cannot have too much of such a very excellent thing." Dots of solder surround the edges and reflect the roundness of the pearls inside. Making an artful chain for it to hang from and tying a snippet from an antique linen book completes this reliquary. I can't wait to wear it!

RELIC ON WHEELS

This whimsical spin on a theme, houses tidbits inside of an antique bottle that I soldered to a set of toy car wheels.

PURPLE RELIQUARY

Antique bottles age in such magical ways. Here, I used a section of a very old bottle that turned violet with age. The flat sides were cut from a piece of violet-stained glass. The color is amazing and I can only imagine how much my grandmother would have loved such a treasure. (Her favorite color was purple.) Nestled inside are playful goodies that capture the tint of the glass. Of course, it dangles from a necklace created from purple beads.

Traditions are the guideposts driven deep in our subconscious minds.
The most powerful ones are those we can't even describe,
aren't even aware of.

Ellen Goodman

MEMORIES-OF-CHRISTMAS
Ornament

THE MAGIC OF THE HOLIDAY SEASON;
a time when tradition is most apparent. My
favorite tradition began as far back as I can
remember—the trek to my grandmother's
("Nanny's") house for Christmas. Her
Christmas tree was always laden with handmade
ornaments collected over the years, each carefully placed just so.
Presents were stacked along the walls, floor to ceiling. Not for just
a few, but for five children and twenty-six grandchildren.

On Christmas Eve, Santa Claus visited the Northeast first, so
our stockings were filled by the stroke of midnight, and we awoke
to find even more gifts. The house soon filled with laughter as the
entire family celebrated Christmas in the wee, pre-dawn hours. Years later, I
have my own traditions (I secretly dream of someday hosting Christmas in the
middle of the night). Start a handmade tradition of your own, inspired by my
Grandmother and her heirloom tree, by creating ornaments for you and yours
this Christmas and every Christmas thereafter.

ingredients

collage cargo (page 19)

soldering suitcase (page 22)

2 pieces of beveled glass
(I used 1½" x 3" [4cm × 7cm])

matte photo paper

22-gauge wire
(tinned copper or sterling silver)

needle-nose pliers

glass crystal, approx. 1½" (4cm) high

jump rings (7mm or 9mm), 3

6" nickel-plated link chain

Want more?

*Every year, take a picture of your children, your friends, your dog with
Santa. Make this a tradition. Then, each year, create an ornament
using the picture. This can make a beautiful chronology (not to
mention making unpacking the Christmas ornaments more enjoyable).*

1

Using the glass as a template, cut out a photo (or use a colorcopy of one). Here, I left a ¾" (19mm) border at the bottom in order to add a little sentiment. Print text of your choice onto matte photo paper and cut three sides to fit the blank border space at the bottom of the photo. Tear the fourth side (top) and glue it over the blank space. Cut old letters, another photo, or vintage wrapping paper for the back, again using the beveled glass as a guide. Antique this with the charcoal pencil as well. This is a great time to add a personal handwritten message, glue cut-out words from *The Night Before Christmas*, or rubber stamp an initial or special date.

2

Use a charcoal pencil to sketch along the torn paper and smudge with a wet finger to "antique" it. Apply white glue sparingly (with your finger, a brush, or a toothpick) to specific areas on either the front or back artwork (or both) and then sprinkle glass glitter over those areas. Press down with your finger to push the glitter into the glue and shake the glitter off the artwork. Let dry and wipe the excess away. Clean both sides of the glass. Sandwich the artwork, back to back, between the two pieces of beveled glass making sure that the bevels are on the outside. Apply copper tape around all sides of the beveled glass sandwich, making sure that the seam is in the center of the bottom where it will be covered up with solder to hold the crystal in place. Solder and clean. Solder three jump rings to the piece: one to the bottom center (where the seam hopefully is) and two to each side of the top about ¼" (6mm) in from the sides. Clean again and polish.

3

Crystals come in many shapes and sizes. Start with a clean crystal, similar to one of the ones shown here.

4

Remove the hanging hardware from the crystal, using needle-nose pliers. Decide on what portion of your printed tissue you would like cover the crystal with. Apply Diamond Glaze to one side of the crystal.

5

Adhere the tissue.

6

After the glaze has dried, use a wet brush to moisten the perimeter of the crystal, where the excess paper is. Tear the excess paper away.

7

Add another coat of Diamond Glaze over the paper on the crystal to seal it. The finished crystal can be used as-is for a pendant or incorporated into other projects, such as the one we'll use for this holiday ornament. Variations on this technique include adding paint to the back of the crystal, silver leaf, additional text or images and so on.

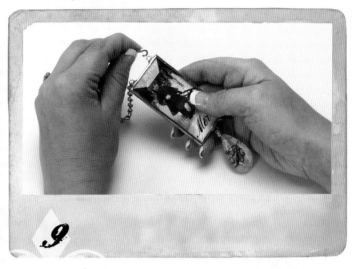

Using only the teardrop part of a teardrop crystal and 22-gauge wire, wire-wrap the crystal to the bottom jump ring. To do this, cut a 6" (15cm) length of wire. Poke the wire through the crystal. Use round-nose pliers to make a loop in the wire about ¼" (6mm) above the crystal and hook the loop through the bottom jump ring. Wrap the loose ends of the wire around and around until the ¼" (6mm) gap is covered. Snip off excess with wire cutters.

Open the end links of the chain and hook through the top jump rings. Use pliers to squeeze the links closed.

Manufacturing Chemists
PHILADELPHIA.

HONOR THY-FATHER ORNAMENT

This very special ornament is made from my favorite photograph. It is my father, long curly locks and all. I can see, even at this age, the sweetness in his eyes. He is a wonderful man with a heart of not just gold, but platinum. I look at the little boy in the photo and I can see each of my children in his face. I wonder if he sat on his grandfather's lap and was read to just like he reads to his grandchildren. The original photograph shares a frame with a photograph of my mother as a teenager and is proudly displayed in my dining room. And I've made small ornaments for each of my children to hang in their bedroom as they should never forget the love that they came from.

A Little More:
MERRY CHRISTMAS GARLAND

I believe in freely showcasing
words, phrases, quotes, and names in
wonderful ways throughout my home.
Giant, old, metal sign letters spell FAMILY
in my living room. Fancy initials hang on the
front of each child's bedroom door. Nearly
all my artwork contains found phrases and
words that provoke laughter or tears.
So, it is no stretch of the imagination that
garland swirling around my Christmas tree
is made from little letters magically tucked
between glass and strung on a shiny silver
chain. Oh, how they sparkle next to the
twinkling white lights! Oh, how they bounce
when the cat bats at them!
Oh, how they are a labor of love!

ingredients

soldering suitcase (see page 22)

1" (3cm) squares of beveled glass, 28

1" (3cm) square prints of letters (such as anagrams)

scraps of paper or copies of old photographs

3' (4m) of link chain

jump rings (6mm), 29

{1} Using one piece of square beveled glass as a template, cut out letters to spell MERRY CHRISTMAS. Each individual letter will be sandwiched between two pieces of glass. The back of the letters may show, so consider adding snippets of text scavenged from old books or copies of photos to the backs of the letters. Clean the glass squares and wrap them in copper tape making sure the seam is on the top center (where the jump ring will go). Do this for all of the letters.

{2} You may wish to add extra charms between the word MERRY and the word CHRISTMAS. This can be done using just a photo behind the glass, an empty charm, or found objects such as icicle ornaments. Solder each charm making sure to attach a jump ring to the top center. Flux, clean and polish.

{3} Use another jump ring to attach each charm to a link in the chain. This will allow the charms to dangle freely and dance about. Don't hesitate to add additional embellishments, beads or charms. For MERRY CHRISTMAS, I added the small round part of a tear-drop crystal.

Ho-Ho Ornament

Vintage anagram game pieces are placed between beveled glass to spell a "HO HO" just in time for the holidays. The longer the phrase, the longer the ornament. Of course, an icicle is formed with a lead glass crystal.

things made of romance and magic

Romance happens. Magic happens. It's not just at the point of pretty.
It's a point beyond—one step further. I can tell when it shows its face.
So can you. You'll notice that little something extra and you'll feel it
inside you.

There's a shrine I made long, long ago. It is meaningful to me as I made it
so long ago and can see what I do today visible in what I did then. To some, it
may be just a box. To others, it may be just pretty. To me, it's meaningful. But
dangling from the little, glass knob used to open it is a fairy ornament, glittered
and chubby in her crepe skirt. Not until I hung the fairy from the knob did it
make the shrine magical. I'm looking at it right now as I write this. I've often
thought of taking that fairy to my studio—after all, I could use a chubby fairy
in a crepe paper skirt there! But I could not take away the magic that she brings
to this shrine, which is, after all, titled "Believe."

It is the addition of something unexpected, beyond the usual, that makes
it magical. A flower is a flower, but with glitter added it is something special.
A doll is just a doll, but with a skirt made of treasures, it's a designer original!
A love note is just a love note, but when encased in glass to have and to
hold forever, it becomes romance captured. A magic wand is a magic wand,
but when it is THIS Magic Wand it is truly . . . magic.

Make magic. Fall in love. You won't be able to resist. But remember,
you won't notice it at first, until you pin the First Place Ribbon on your
daughter that you will say to yourself, oh, yes, that is magical. Or when
you hang Love Notes on your bedpost. Oh, yes, that is romantic.

Love is everything.   It is the key to life,   and its influences are those that move the world.

Ralph Waldo Trine

LOVE
Notes

How do I love thee? Let me count the ways. I love thee till I mistakenly cut up important bills and letters just to create love notes. I love thee till I burn my fingers soldering these pieces together. I love thee even more when I get a Love Note in return! Capture your love forever with a Love Note that every postman would love to deliver, only these are notes you will want to hand over in person. It's like sending your heart in the mail, only better—extra postage is NOT required.

ingredients

collage cargo (see page 19)

soldering suitcase (see page 22)

heart-shaped, beveled glass, 2 (available at many stained-glass stores)

16-gauge wire (tinned copper or sterling silver), 3"–4" (8cm–10cm)

wire cutters

round-nose pliers

Want more?

Write Love Notes to your husband and children. Surprise them by hanging them on their doorknobs on Valentine's Day. Have them write you Love Notes in return. Solder them to create jewelry and proudly wear them around your neck. Always start and end the day by saying "I love you"—and mean it.

Using the glass heart as a guide, cut out antique letters in the shape of the heart glass for the background of your collage. Make sure to include the stamp. If the paper you're cutting doesn't have a stamp, add one!

2

Cut out text from vintage books to convey the message you wish to send. Messages can be silly or sentimental. Here, I've said, "I love you more than you will ever know but wish you would take out the trash." Some of this text I found "as-is," some I gave creative license to! Place the completed artwork between the two pieces of clean glass, making sure the beveled edges are on the outside. Beginning just off to the side of the center top, apply copper tape (here I have used ½" [13mm]) all around the edge of the heart, making sure to overlap the spot where the two ends of tape meet. Carefully fold the copper tape over to both the front and back. Where there is curvature, you will have overlaps and creases. Burnish smooth.

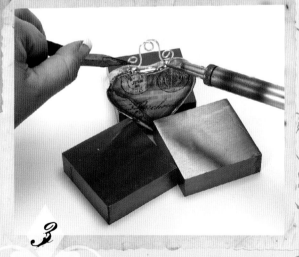

3

Solder all the copper-taped areas. Either prop up the hearts or hold them with pliers. Clean and polish. Use round-nose pliers to create loops in the wire to form the handle. The swirls can be as simple or ornate as you desire. Prop the heart upright. Flux the wire and the soldered edge of the heart where they will meet. Holding the wire with pliers, solder the wire to the heart. Clean and polish.

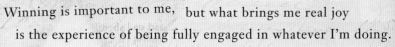

Winning is important to me, but what brings me real joy
is the experience of being fully engaged in whatever I'm doing.

Phil Jackson

Pin

GROWING UP, SOME
THINGS WERE ALWAYS A
LITTLE ASKEW. On my birthday, my father
wouldn't say "*Happy Birthday*," he would say "*Happy
Bastille Day*," since I was born on Bastille Day (the French Fourth
of July). He also called me his "favorite daughter," which, of course,
prompted me to reply "But I'm your *only* daughter." This began when
I was young and blonde—and eventually I understood the humor in it.
Of course, I've always yearned for "favorite child" status, but my brother
had something to say about that! I am proud to pass on the tradition to
my daughter—my *only* daughter, who is also my "favorite daughter."

ingredients

collage cargo (see page 19)

soldering suitcase (see page 22)

1/16" (2mm) window glass,
approximately 1¾" × ½"
(4cm × 13mm), 2

beveled, round glass
approximately 1½" (4cm) in
diameter, 2

pin back

jump rings
    (7mm or 8mm), 4
    (5mm or 6mm), 2 to 4

1" to 1½" (3cm to 4cm) ribbon,
about 12" (30cm)

epoxy

1

Select a special photograph to go inside the beveled circle. (The photograph should have a matte finish.) Create your artwork to go inside both the round glass and the rectangular glass. Trim the artwork to fit. When creating your artwork, keep in mind that a portion of the back of the rectangular piece will be covered with the pin finding, and a portion of the back of the round piece will be covered with ribbon.

Clean the glass and sandwich the artwork between the glass. Wrap copper tape around the rim making sure to fold over equally on both the front and back. Solder the copper-taped areas.

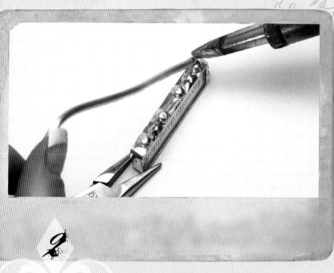

2

Use the "dot" technique (see page 35) to add decorative solder dots all around the rectangular and round pieces.

3

Add jump rings. The placement of the jump rings on the round piece (at the top) should be equal to, or slightly narrower than, the placement of the jump rings on the rectangular piece (at the bottom). Clean and polish. Connect the rectangular piece to the round piece with one or two smaller jump rings.

4

Glue the pin finding to the back of the rectangular piece using epoxy. (Note: The pin back opening should face down, just in case it should open when wearing it.) Let dry. Cut the length of ribbon in half and use epoxy to attach the ribbon to the back of the round glass near the bottom. You will need to lay out the ribbon at an angle and then cut it straight (so as to not cover up too much artwork). Let it dry and then trim the ends to mimic an actual first-place ribbon.

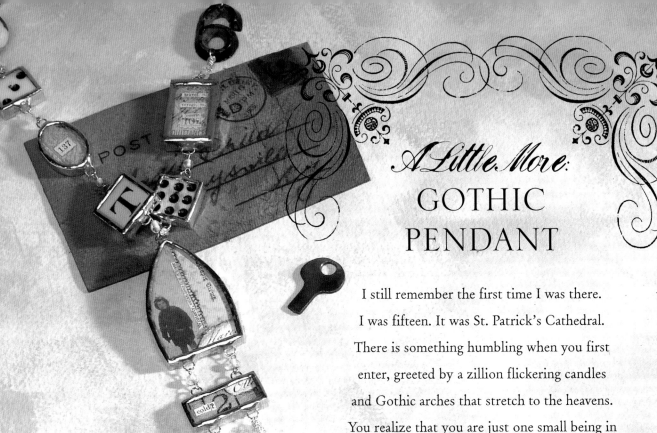

A Little More: GOTHIC PENDANT

I still remember the first time I was there. I was fifteen. It was St. Patrick's Cathedral. There is something humbling when you first enter, greeted by a zillion flickering candles and Gothic arches that stretch to the heavens. You realize that you are just one small being in all of humanity. As I stood under the arches, tears welling up in my eyes, I grasped what that meant. I also understood that I would never forget that moment. The beauty of it. The grace. I hold that spiritual side close to my heart. I am drawn to that shape, Gothic arches. I paid dearly for a chippy-paint chair with a rare Gothic arch on the back. I covet old Gothic windows, their only purpose now is to lean against the wall and let one daydream of views seen through them long ago. When creating this new pendant, I found myself grinding a piece of rectangular glass while my mind wandered. The next thing I knew, there they were, the Gothic arches I have loved for so long. It may sound bizarre, but somehow that glass shape came from a place deep within me.

ingredients

collage cargo (see page 19)

soldering suitcase (see page 22)

rectangular glass approximately 1¼" × 2" (3cm × 5cm), 2

rectangular glass approximately 1⅛" × ½" (3cm × 13mm), 2

jump rings, (7mm), 7

assorted beads, 4

found objects (here we used an old key and a silver bumblebee charm)

20-gauge wire (tinned copper wire or sterling silver wire)

{1} Grind the large pair of rectangles using an electric grinder into a gothic shape. Many stained-glass stores allow you to use their equipment, or they will grind it for you, for a small fee. Create artwork that will go inside both the large gothic shape and the smaller rectangle. Use the glass as your guide to cut the artwork to the same size and shape as the glass.

{2} Clean the glass and tape both pairs. The seams should be where the jump rings will go (as the excess solder for the jump rings will hide the seam). Solder both pieces. To the gothic piece, add a jump ring on the top at the point. Add two jump rings, one on each side, to the bottom.

{3} To the smaller rectangle, solder two jump rings to the top (line up the jump rings with the bottom of the gothic piece), and two to the bottom. You may add more jump rings if you want more trinkets to hang from the bottom. Flux clean and polish both pieces.

{4} Using a 4" (10cm) length of wire, create a loop ½" (13mm) beyond the center point. Feed the loop through one of the bottom jump rings on the gothic shape. Twist the wire to secure it in place. Then, feed a bead onto the wire and create a loop on the bead's other side. Feed that loop through the corresponding top jump ring of the rectangle shape and twist the wire around it. Repeat for the other side.

{5} Cut two more 4" pieces of wire for attaching the found objects. First, create a loop about ½" from the center of the wire and feed it through the bottom jump ring of the smaller rectangular piece. Twist the end around to secure it in place. Then feed a bead onto the wire and create another loop beyond that. Feed that loop onto your found object and twist it around to secure it in place. Attach your chain (in this case, our Found Object Chain) jump ring at the top of the gothic shape.

Wondrous Necklace

Wondrousness. It's a twelve-letter word that describes this labor of love. A word on each charm spells a phrase found in an old book: "Make me happy, if only for a little while. And soothe me." Each is tied together by hand-wrapping sterling wire with found pearls (this is where the labor of love part comes in). Surely a showpiece, this necklace is red-carpet worthy. Jennifer Lopez, eat your heart out!

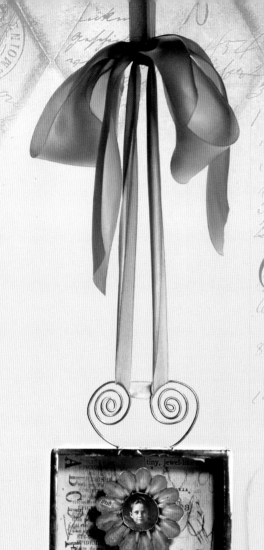

I hope that while so many people are out smelling the flowers,
someone is taking the time to plant some.

Herbert Rappaport

FLOWER-BOX
Shrine

I KILL PLASTIC PLANTS. That's how atrocious my gardening skills are. My rosemary—mites within a week. Roses my husband brings me— wilt within an hour. The only things I grow in my garden are dandelions (my "garden" primarily being the cracks in the concrete). This is all quite tragic because I love, love, love flowers. So, when God gives you a black thumb, make lemonade! Or, rather, make flower box shrines! That's what I did. Just imagine a garden of your own—growing the flowers you see in your dreams. Never needing to water them, yet they bloom all year long!

ingredients

collage cargo (see page 19)

soldering suitcase (see page 22)

square jewelry box (4" × 4" × 1" [10cm × 10cm × 3cm] was used here)

1/16" (2mm) window glass

contact paper (for stenciling)

glass etching cream

sponge brush

jump rings (6mm), 2

small river stone

16-gauge wire (tinned copper), about 12" (30cm)

wire cutters

round-nose pliers

Want more?

Cardboard jewelry boxes aren't just for jewelry anymore. Forget the diamond ring that came inside—use the box to create a shrine you will cherish even more! And why stop at jewelry boxes—shoe boxes, mayonnaise jar lids, the metal spout from a box of dishwasher detergent! The possibilities for planting dimensional gems are endless!

1

Start with a square jewelry box and collage the inside of the box with acrylic paint and paper ephemera, adhered with gel medium. Use a heat gun to dry everything well and remove excess moisture. Next, add three-dimensional objects. I like to use caulk to secure objects for the best staying power. Make sure each object you put inside the box isn't deeper than the box itself, or the glass will not lie flat on top.

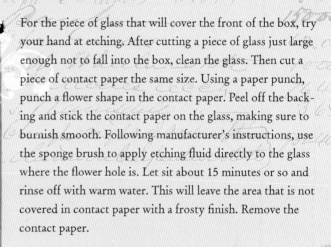

2

For the piece of glass that will cover the front of the box, try your hand at etching. After cutting a piece of glass just large enough not to fall into the box, clean the glass. Then cut a piece of contact paper the same size. Using a paper punch, punch a flower shape in the contact paper. Peel off the backing and stick the contact paper on the glass, making sure to burnish smooth. Following manufacturer's instructions, use the sponge brush to apply etching fluid directly to the glass where the flower hole is. Let sit about 15 minutes or so and rinse off with warm water. This will leave the area that is not covered in contact paper with a frosty finish. Remove the contact paper.

4

After the box is wrapped, flux and solder the entire box. Because there is a large surface area to fill, hold the solder coil to the iron and melt several drops over the side of the box, then use the iron to spread the solder around.

3

Dry the glass with a paper towel. Cut a second piece of glass the same size as the back of the box. Clean both pieces of glass. Place one piece on the back of the box, over the flat artwork you created. To keep the glass in place, add four dots of Diamond Glaze in the four corners and press it to the box. Allow the adhesive to dry before doing the same thing to the other side. Cut a piece of copper sheet the width of the box plus ⅜" (10mm) on each side and the sum total of each side of the box plus ½" (13mm). For example, for a box that is 4" × 4"× 1", the copper tape will be 1¾" × 16½". Wrap the box with the copper foil tape. For this project, I put the seam at the center bottom (which will be covered up with a jump ring). Carefully burnish smooth.

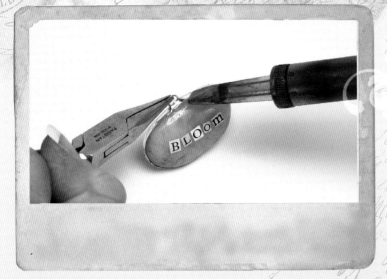

5

Tack-solder a jump ring to the bottom of the box. Add artwork to a stone. Here, I cut out individual letters to spell BLOOM and used caulk to adhere them directly to the stone. Cut a strip of copper tape to about ¼" (6mm) wide. Wrap the stone with the copper tape, allowing the seam to be at the top center. Burnish smooth. Solder the tape to the stone, and add a jump ring to the top center.

6

Using round-nose pliers, twirl a length of 16-gauge wire into two swirls at each end with the center length between them being about 2" (5cm) of flattened wire. Use pliers to hold this in place (centered on the top of the box) and solder in place by soldering over the flattened wire. Clean and polish the entire piece including the soldered areas of the stone. Feed a length of ribbon through the jump ring of the stone and then through the bottom jump ring on the box allowing for a bit of length so it can hang. The excess ribbon looks artful as it dangles. Feed each end of the ribbon through the twisted wire from the back to the front, and tie in a bow about 4" (10cm) or so above the twisted wire. Trim the ribbon to a length you like and hang the piece.

VOCABULARY

Sometimes other objects are the focal point, and the shrine is merely icing on the cake—as it is with Vocabulary, a printer's block that showcases a small shrine atop it. Both pieces are soldered together and carefully hung from a stand that held an antique mirror in its previous life.

STRAWBERRY DROP FAIRY

Life is not complete without bartender, Bob's special Strawberry Drop (found only at the Paragon Restaurant, in Portland, Oregon). Also known as "mommy-koolaid," this delicious drink has inspired many an idea! To show my appreciation, I created the Strawberry Drop Fairy so everyone can have one! Game pieces for feet, velvety strawberries inside, and Bob's special recipe on the back . . .no one can have just one Strawberry Drop! Especially not me!

THE CIRCUS PERFORMER

The playful movement of a circus trapeze is captured within this shrine complete with a vintage child's tray cut up to form the sides of the box. The circa 1800s antique porcelain doll actually swings on her own trapeze. A spring becomes the hanger through which red silk ribbon is strung.

The universe is full of magical things,

patiently waiting for our wits to grow sharper.

Eden Phillpotts

MAGIC
Wand

IMAGINE HAVING A
MAGIC WAND. Would
you wave it and make the
laundry go away? Would you
wave it so your teenagers would wake
up before 11A.M. on the weekend?
Would you wave it to lose ten pounds?
Would you wave it only to have a million
dollars appear in your silverware drawer?
Or, would you wave it and cure incurable diseases?
Would you wave it to eliminate world hunger? Would you
wave it for peace on earth? Make your very own magic
wand. Close your eyes, wave it and believe in the magic.

ingredients

collage cargo (see page 19)

soldering suitcase (see page 22)

round beveled glass, 2" (5cm) diameter, 2

diamond-shaped, beveled glass, 6

16-gauge wire

wire cutters

round-nose pliers

glass drops (that have been collaged
and soldered [see page 23]), 4

18" (46cm) length of solid
acrylic rod (square or round)

Want more?

*If you can't find an acrylic rod for the wand staff, substitute
a metal rod, wooden dowel, branch, or anything your
imagination finds suitable.*

1

Score the flat side of the diamond shapes and, using breakers, snap them in half. Grind the corners smooth. You will use five of these triangles for this project.

Create artwork (original paper or prints made with waterproof ink) to go behind each of the five triangles. Apply Diamond Glaze to the flat side of a triangle. Press the artwork into it and burnish smooth. Apply several more coats to the back of the artwork, allowing each coat to dry before applying the next. Repeat for the other four triangles. Create a two-sided piece of artwork to go inside the round, beveled glass. Clean the glass and sandwich the finished artwork inside. Wrap the triangles and the circle with copper tape. Seam the copper tape on the bottom of each shape. Burnish smooth. Solder each piece individually.

Place the center top triangle piece above the round piece (making sure that it is centered and straight). Tack solder it into place. Continue doing this with the remaining four triangles, leaving room at the center bottom for the rod. Flip the pieces over and tack-solder the back. Flip the piece face up again and do a nice, smooth solder where the triangles connect to the round piece.

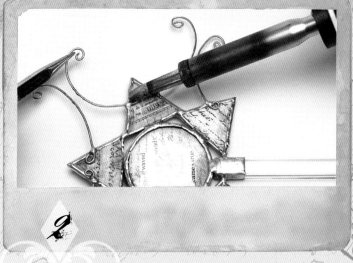

2

Wrap both ends of the acrylic rod with copper tape and burnish smooth. Solder the ends making sure to stop often to allow the acrylic to cool (as it could melt). Place one end of the soldered acrylic tube up against the round shape in the open space. Solder this in place (it should be soldered to both the round piece and the triangles on each of its sides). Clean and polish. Cut the wire into ten 6" (15cm) lengths and bend each to a nice curve. Use round-nose pliers to loop both ends. Apply flux, and tack solder one end of each curved wire about halfway up the sides of each triangle back, as shown.

3

Lay soldered glass drops face down underneath two of the curved wire pieces. Apply flux and solder these in place. (Note: To keep the glass drops from moving, lay them on a small piece of double-stick tape.) Continue this for all four glass drops.

Cut eight lengths of wire to 2½" (6cm). Bend the wire in half and twist the ends as shown, into a V shape. Use pliers to hold the wire in place and solder them to the backs of the glass drops. Clean and polish all areas where it has been soldered.

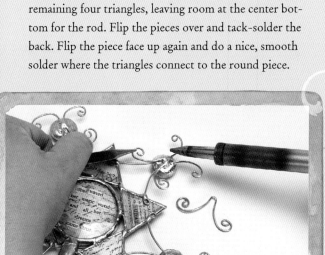

4

TOTALLY Tiara

Think like a queen. A queen is not afraid to fail. Failure is another stepping-stone to greatness.

Oprah Winfrey

SHE'S A PRINCESS. No, on second thought, she's a queen! She wears a crown on her head while doing the dishes. She has one for every day of the week. Her children bow in her presence. Her husband worships the ground she walks on. Her boss lets her come in late and leave early. Even her cat saves the hairballs until after she's left the room. She's a queen—and she's dreaming—but, if she had her very own crown perhaps it would help her live that dream. Even if it was only a *day*-dream.

ingredients

collage cargo (see page 19)

soldering suitcase (see page 22)

game pieces such as anagrams that spell a special sentiment (optional: dominos cut in half, Scrabble game pieces, or flat, square objects), approximately 17

cardstock scrap

mounting tape

diamond-shaped beveled glass pieces, 9

16-gauge wire

20-gauge wire

wire cutters

round-nose pliers

crystals, beads and found objects for embellishment (optional)

Want more?

As a surprise, make a tiara for your very best friend. Spell her name on the front, spell her nickname on the back. Put copies of her baby pictures in each of the triangles. Dangle decorated crystals from the silvery spirals. Wrap it up in a cake box with pink tissue paper (don't forget to tie it with red-and-white wax ribbon). Give it to her when she's not expecting it. Make her wear it out in public. She is a queen, after all!

1

Apply copper tape around the anagram game pieces. (Glass is not necessary.) The seam should be at the top, as it will be covered up by the beveled triangles.

2

Solder each game piece separately. Clean and polish. Draw an oval on a piece of cardstock. To determine the size of the oval, use a piece of wire and wrap it around your head. Trace the outline of that wire on paper. Since this tiara has some sections in between the squares that contain wire, there is an opportunity before adding the triangles to adjust the shape and size of the tiara and better form it to your head. Place mounting tape over the drawn line all the way around the oval.

3

Arrange the soldered squares on-end, on the double-stick tape. Butt them up against one another, leaving a space between words should you desire. (This is where spirals of wire can go.) When arranging the letters, keep in mind that the center-front of the tiara should feature the most important word, centered.

4

Apply flux and tack solder the squares together where they meet at the top.

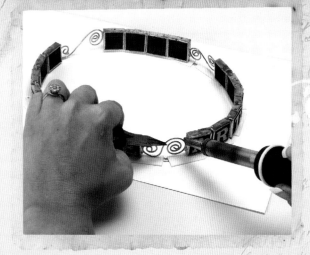

5

Use round-nose pliers to twirl the ends of 16-gauge wire and create decorative swirls. The swirls should be no higher than the squares. Tack-solder the wire swirls to the squares to fill the gaps.

Gently peel the tiara off the double-stick tape. Try the tiara on and see if it fits. You may adjust the shape by carefully bending and shaping the tiara with your hands. Try it on for circumference at this point. If it needs to be tighter, twirl the wire a little more and then solder it into place. If it needs to be looser, untwirl the wire some. Flip the base of the tiara over and tack-solder the underside of all the squares. Clean and polish. Score the center back (flat side) of the beveled diamonds. Use breakers to snap the diamonds in half to form triangles. Gently grind the corners of the triangles. (You will need about 15 triangles, but the quantity depends on the size of your tiara.)

6

7

Apply Diamond Glaze to the flat side of your triangle and press artwork against it. Rub it smooth and let dry. Apply several coats of Diamond Glaze over the back of the artwork to seal it, allowing it to dry between coats. Wrap the triangles with copper tape making sure the seam is at the bottom. Carefully fold the corners over and burnish smooth. Solder these individually, then clean and polish each one.

1

Begin the doll body by making rings with 16-gauge wire with diameters of: 1½", 2½", 3¾", 5", 6", and 6½" (4cm, 6cm, 10cm, 13cm, 15cm and 17cm).

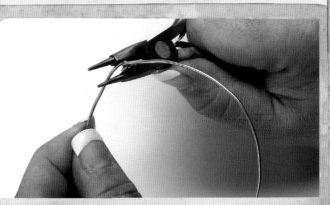

3

Apply flux and solder the connection of each ring, so they remain firm.

2

Use round-nose pliers to create a hook on each end of the wire rings and hook (join) them together, pinching the hooked ends tightly.

4

When you are finished creating the 6 rings, cut six lengths of the same wire that are about 10" (25cm). Use round-nose pliers to make a hook in just one end of the wire. Straighten the wire using needle-nose pliers and/or a burnishing stick.

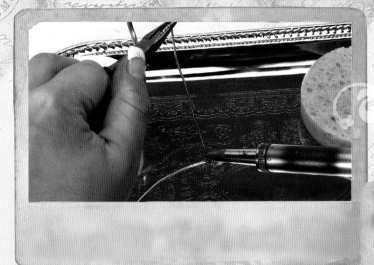

5

Lay the largest ring down and hook one of the straight wires to it. Use needle-nose pliers to squeeze it together. Apply flux and solder the connection. (Make sure to hold the wire with pliers, as it can get hot.)

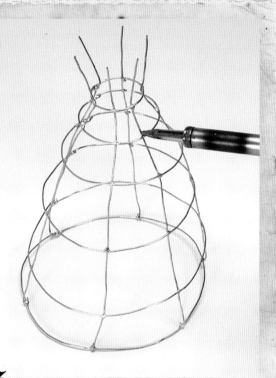

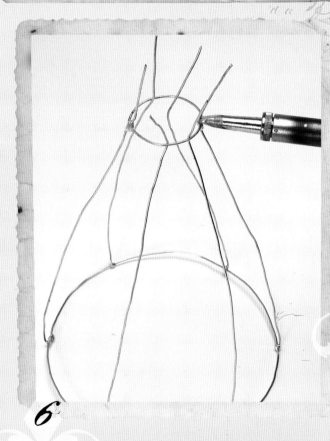

6

Solder another piece of wire in the same manner directly across from the first. Do this for all six straight pieces of wire making sure that they are evenly spaced from one another. In the perfect world of the clock, this would mean attaching straight pieces at noon and 6:00, 10:00, 4:00, 2:00 and 8:00. Thread the smallest ring onto the six straight pieces, allowing about 1½" (4cm) of the straight pieces to stick out from the top. Use pliers to hold the ring in place. Apply flux and solder it to each of the six straight pieces.

7

Thread the next smallest ring onto the six straight pieces and attach in the same manner. Continue doing this until all the rings are used, keeping the soldered joints of the rings aligned. Clean the flux and polish. You are now ready to begin embellishing the skirt form. By the way, aren't you glad we don't actually wear skirts with metal forms anymore?

8

Gather an assortment of velvet leaves with wire stems. Pull the leaves apart so they are single leaves with stems.

9

Use acrylic paint to alter the color of the velvet leaves. The paint does not need to completely cover each leaf. Add paint to the back of the leaf as well. Let dry.

Rub caulk on the leaf where you'd like to collage. Tear a bit of vintage paper and apply it to the caulked area, pressing down to adhere it. Let dry.

10

11

Apply dabs of white glue to the edges of the velvet leaves.

12

Dip the leaves in a bowl of glitter. (Here I've used a silver German glass glitter, which will tarnish with age.)

13

Let dry and shake off the excess.

14

Cut a strip of copper tape to the length of the first leaf stem. Lay the stem on the copper tape and roll it up tightly. Apply flux to the copper tape and solder it, making sure to cover all the areas of the copper tape. Clean and polish. Do this for all the leaves.

15

Hold the leaves and apply flux to the leaf and the doll form where you want them to connect. Solder the leaf to the form. Clean the flux and polish the soldered areas as you go. Use round-nose pliers to carefully create curves and loops in your stem (as shown), should the mood strike you.

Continue adding leaves going in all directions until the form is well covered. Add decorative trim to the bottom of the form, if you desire. To do this, apply copper tape to the top rim and fold it over the edge. Burnish and solder it. Apply flux and tack solder it to the bottom-most ring. After it is entirely attached, trim any excess and go back to add a final, smooth coat of solder. Clean and polish it when it is completely attached. Use Diamond Glaze to apply tiny snippets of words cut out of old books. Brush Diamond Glaze on the wire frame or the metal trim, press the cut-out text into it and let dry. Seal with another brushing of Diamond Glaze.

16

Shopping with Sally

If you want to make things just like Sally does, you have to know where to shop!
Consult the following web sites to find exactly what you need:

AMERIGLAS STAINED GLASS
(Diamond Drill & Tool Division)
www.diamond-drill-bit-and-tool.com
glass saw

CANFIELD TECHNOLOGIES
www.canfieldmetals.com
solder

CLINE GLASS COMPANY
www.clineglasscompany.com
glass, glass supplies

EBAY
www.ebay.com
*vintage ledgers, bunny slippers and
everything else under the sun*

FIRE MOUNTAIN GEMS
www.firemountaingems.com
sterling silver supplies, beads

GLASTAR CORPORATION
www.glastar.com
glass grinder

PAPIER VALISE
www.papiervalise.com
*porcelain letters, silver wings, tiny treasures,
found objects*

PARAGON RESTAURANT & BAR
www.paragonrestaurant.com
*strawberry drops (exclusively in Portland, OR),
gorgonzola cheesecake, rosemary fries*

RIO GRANDE
www.riogrande.com
sterling silver supplies, gemstones, metalsmith tools

SALLY JEAN
www.sallyjean.com
vintage art collage charms, pre-cut glass, glass supplies

SPECTRUM
www.freedomcrystal.com
assorted crystals (chandelier-type)

STELLAR TECHNICAL PRODUCTS
www. stellartechnical.com
gel flux

TORTOISE ORCHARD
www.tortoiseorchard.safeshopper.com
German glass glitter

COOPER INDUSTRIES, LLC
(Cooper Hand Tools Division/Weller)
www.cooperhandtools.com/brands/weller/index.cfm
soldering iron

Index

Who is Sally Jean, anyway?

ONCE UPON A TIME, THERE WAS A VERY SILLY GIRL WHO LIVED IN A BIG CASTLE WITH TURRETS THAT REACHED HIGH INTO COTTON CANDY CLOUDS.

WILBUR & HASTINGS-27646

Sally Jean is a self-taught, mixed-media artist who, frankly, has ants in her pants. Throughout her entire life, she has dabbled, experimented and basically made a mess in all kinds of mediums. From early drawings on luggage to hand-formed pottery to the now all-the-rage Art Collage Charms, she couldn't stop crafting new things. After taking the plunge from a longtime career in real estate into art, she has found a way to mix all her silly obsessions into a successful art enterprise. Her Vintage Art Collage Charms, which she began making in 1999, can be found at boutiques and in private collections all over the world. She has been featured in *Oregon Home* magazine and *Somerset Studio*. Her work has appeared in *Romantic Homes* magazine, *Mary Engelbreit's Home Companion* magazine, as well as *Cloth Paper Scissors* magazine, and WB's "Extra" for her Paula Abdul Tiara! She teaches her techniques to make irresistible projects at workshops throughout the United States and abroad.

Although her heart is in her New England upbringing, she currently lives in Portland, Oregon, with her husband Brad ("Mr. Sally Jean" as he likes to be called—on occasion) and her three children Elliott, Erika and Enzo. She loves her life, where she can stay in bunny slippers all day and they've learned not to mind her green-painted fingertips at the grocery store. She starts her day watching the sun rise over Mount Hood and ends it curled up on a fluffy chair with a fire going (even in the summer), sharing the day's events with her children. Between sunrise and sunset, you will find her dancing while she's painting, singing while she's soldering, and twirling. Always twirling.

Visit Sally at her Website:
WWW.SALLYJEAN.COM

Want more?

SALLY'S BIGGEST FEAR?
That someday the world will run out of old, tintype albums. Really, I mean, how many flashcards does one girl need?

WHO DOES SALLY ADMIRE?
Women who think for themselves. People who don't take themselves too seriously. Her grandmother.

p.127

JOSIE CIRINCIONE

Inside *Collage Lost and Found*, you'll learn how to find and use old photographs, memorabilia and ephemera to create collages based on your heritage. Using her own Sicilian background as an example, author Josie Cirincione shows you how to examine your own heritage for inspiration, as well as tips on where to look and what to look for. Then you'll choose from 20 step-by-step projects that use basic collage, jewelry-making and image transfer techniques to make sassy projects to decorate with, wear and give away as gifts.

ISBN-10: 1-58180-787-2

ISBN-13: 978-1-58180-787-5

paperback 128 pages 33461

CLAUDINE HELLMUTH

In a follow-up to her first workshop book, Claudine Hellmuth taps into a whole new level of creativity in *Beyond the Unexpected*. Inside you'll find original artwork and inventive ideas that show you how to personalize your own collage pieces using new techniques and interesting surfaces. In addition, the extensive gallery compiled by Claudine and other top collage artists will spark your imagination. Whether you're a beginner or a collage veteran, you'll enjoy this lovely book both as inspiration and as a practical guide.

ISBN 10: 1-58180-535-7

ISBN 13: 978-1-58180-535-2

paperback 128 pages 33267

LINDA & OPIE O'BRIEN

Discover a nontraditional approach to the introduction of working with metal as you create 20 fun and funky projects. This is the whimsical side of metal that not only teaches you how to cut and join metal surfaces, but also allows you to explore ways to age and add texture to metal, conjure up beautiful patina finishes and uncover numerous types of metal such as copper, mesh, wire and recycled material. Whether you've worked with metal before or you're new to the medium, give your recyled tin cans a second glance and start crafting beautiful pieces with metal today.

ISBN-10: 1-58180-646-9

ISBN-13: 978-1-58180-646-5

paperback 128 pages 33235

LINDA WOODS & KAREN DININO

Have you always wanted to dive into art journaling, but you're always stopped by what to put on the page? Finally, there is a book that comes to your rescue! Visual Chronicles is your no-fear guide to expressing your deepest self with words as art, and artful words. You'll learn quick ways to chronicle your thoughts with painting, stamping, collaging and writing. Friendly projects like the Personal Palette and the Mini Prompt Journal make starting easy. You'll also find inspiration for experimenting with colors, shapes, ephemera, communicating styles, symbols and more!

ISBN-10: 1-58180-770-8

ISBN-13: 978-1-58180-770-7

paperback 128 pages 33442